the BOND *we* SHARE

A True Story of Adoption, Family Dysfunction, Traumatic Separation, and the Healing Journey That Reunited a Brother and Sister

PATRICK | *Melyssa*
Butler | FLEMING

M&P BOND PUBLISHING

Cover image: Dina Turco / Dina Turco Photography
Cover Graphic Design and Layout: Lindsey Pillow
Thank you both for your amazing work.
Your talents helped to bring our vision to life

www.MandPBondPublishing.com

Hardcover: 979-8-9906272-1-5
Paperback: 979-8-9906272-2-2
Kindle: 979-8-9906272-3-9

Production by Concierge Marketing Inc., www.conciergemarketing.com

Printed in the United States of America
10 9 8 7 6 5 4 3 2 1

KINTSUGI

Kintsugi is a Japanese art of repair that involves using gold or silver pigment to reassemble shattered pottery vessels. In much the same way, we can acknowledge and embrace our imperfections. The parts of us that are broken can heal and become stronger and even more beautiful as we mend. We can grow from our experiences and lead a more valuable life as we make ourselves whole again.

CONTENTS

TWENTY-FOUR YEARS

A lot can happen in twenty-four years. For example:

- ◆ A child can be born, enter grade school, complete middle and high school, and graduate from college.
- ◆ Half of most people's careers can be completed.
- ◆ Six presidential terms can come and go.
- ◆ Twenty-four football seasons and Super Bowls can be played.
- ◆ Technology can make tremendous advances, such as switching from VCRs to Blu-Ray disc players and from floppy disks to cloud storage.

The twenty-four years that are the focus of this book took place from 1981 to 2005.

During that span, the definition of "family" that my sister and I believed in was shattered, shifted, and redefined. This particular period of time began when we were children and ended when we were in our thirties.

In our case, the things that happened within that time span included twenty-four years' worth of birthdays, holidays, high school graduations, weddings, and the birth of children, as well as every ordinary moment in between that would otherwise have been taken for granted.

It is our history, and it played a vital role in shaping who we have become. That sounds obvious, right? Of course the years of your life have shaped who you are now.

You might think that most siblings go through many of the same life experiences that we did. You would be right in saying that, but you would be omitting one important detail. When we experienced all of those events we were separated from each other, and not for a reason that you might assume. We didn't get to witness each other experience any of those moments.

We were robbed of that opportunity. It took twenty-four years for us to reconnect and a few more to understand why the separation had happened. After many years of talking about what had happened, we decided to write down what we knew as well as what we have discovered along the way.

We have written this book for us, for our families, and for our friends.

As we shared our story with friends, many of them told us, "You should write a book!" Saying that you want to write a book about your life can sound good when you are talking with friends over drinks. However, sitting down and beginning the process is a daunting task if you have never done such a thing before!

With scattered notes in hand those writing sessions began, and little by little we pieced our story together.

You are now holding those collected words. We have compiled our story to the best of our ability.

It is time for us to shed light on those twenty-four years apart and quite a bit more.

From here on out, P = Patrick and M = Melyssa

P
1970 PLUS A FEW

I was born in 1970 in Omaha, Nebraska. My family was by all accounts a true-blue working-class family from the Midwest. My father Earl was an auto mechanic, and my mother Beth worked as an aide in the elementary school that I attended.

Earl was born in Iowa and Beth in Nebraska. They met, married, and settled in Omaha, Nebraska, a city that is near the border between the two states. With both of their extended families in Omaha or within a two-hour drive, it was easy to have family gatherings.

Childhood friends of my parents lived in a newly developed neighborhood, and it was a simple choice for my parents to choose the same development for their own home. Because of that, I was fortunate to have friends my age who lived on my block. They were my first friends in life and thankfully remain close to me to this day. As we grew up, my friends and I played outside until the streetlights came on and then ran home to have dinner with our families. Our parents would gather for cookouts and would watch each other's kids while errands were run. It was the picture of an ideal Midwestern neighborhood.

People looked out for each other, and we never had a concern about anyone. Our lives were similar to those of countless families throughout the country and seemed about as normal as you could find if you looked at us from the outside.

I was the first child born into our family, and my parents hoped to add another. After a few years of trying for a second child, my mother was unable to get pregnant. Everything tested out okay, but for some reason my mother just couldn't conceive. This led them to pursue other options.

My parents had been attending a Baptist church for many years, and through friends in the church they found an adoption agency that had been used by other families. After the paperwork and pre-screening had been completed, my parents waited patiently to hear from the agency. Finally, a match was made! The Holt Adoption Agency matched Earl and Beth with a baby girl who had been abandoned and put into a foster home. At the time of her adoption, she was only six weeks old. Adding a new member to our family was great news except for the fact that my parents couldn't drive down the street to pick her up. She wasn't close to Omaha at all—she was in Korea.

After the proper arrangements were made, the process was in full swing. My sister began her journey from Korea to her new home in the United States by taking a long flight with a chaperone. To complete the journey to our home, she had to be picked up in Minneapolis, Minnesota. My dad made the 380-mile drive on his own while my mother stayed with me back home.

Dad loaded up our Ford LTD and made the seven-hour drive north for the connection. The official exchange was made at the airport, and after everything was completed, my dad put my sister in the car and headed home. The biggest detail that my dad shared with me about that day was that he had to drive through pouring rain on the way home. He remembered navigating through a torrential downpour while attempting to keep an infant calm for hours on end. I would have liked to have seen how things went with a one-month-old baby in tow while making that drive back!

"Myung Ae Noh" was the name given to my sister in Korea. After being adopted by my parents, she was given the name "Melyssa Dawn Butler."

Just like that, we became a family of four overnight. I was two and a half years old at that point, so I was excited to have a new playmate. As I look at family photos from this period I see two kids who are truly having fun with each other. There are posed photos taken at portrait studios like Olan Mills and JC Penney that are more formal, and there are candid shots taken at various family get-togethers and holiday celebrations. Many of the candid photos have a common theme: two children having fun and just being kids. Most, if not all, of the photos were taken in our home or at the home of one of our grandparents.

As I study the photos now, I look closely at the faces of all the people who have been captured in each frame. I look at us as kids, of course, but then I study the adults in the photos. Their facial expressions seem happy and normal by all accounts. They don't show any signs that anything was out of the ordinary. Quite the opposite, actually. You see a family that is laughing, talking, and enjoying whatever moment they were in. The photos show us from infancy through early grade school. There are several taken at family Christmas gatherings or dressed up in our Easter best, as well as many fun birthday parties with friends. It is common now to take photos daily, but back then it typically happened only on special occasions.

Each photo captures a moment in time, and more often than not it was a happy one. Unfortunately, the photos don't tell the entire story. I have looked at them thousands of times in an effort to understand what my parents or extended family were thinking when the photos were taken. I have scrutinized each photo carefully, trying to find a hidden clue that might reveal the challenges my parents were beginning to deal with. Many years later, I learned that from the onset of my sister's arrival, my parents had faced challenges they didn't expect. When my sister entered our household, my parents felt nothing but joy initially. Their workload doubled, however, and that can be stressful in the beginning. It is tough enough to be a young parent, but even tougher when you add a second child overnight. The good news is that the excitement and love you feel can reduce the stress a bit as you try to find a new rhythm in your household. All of that is normal for new parents. My parents had been dealing with the changes as best they could until a new level of stress was added that they didn't expect.

When you have children, you expect your extended family to be supportive and show love for each child regardless of how your family grew. In our case we added a family member through adoption. If the extended family suddenly doubted the parents' decision to adopt after the baby had arrived, the adoptive parents would feel a whole new level of stress and anxiety. That surprising twist was not what my parents had expected, but it is what they received, and that is where things started to unravel.

𝓟

WORDS CAN CUT DEEP

Typically, when a couple has a newborn, they are surrounded by family and friends who shower them with good wishes. This would be a natural reaction upon seeing a beautiful baby. In most cases, the closest family members are the people who provide the strongest support. They are there to prepare meals, to help around the house, or possibly to keep your older toddler busy so you can focus on your baby. At the very least, you would expect that when they spoke to you, the members of your extended family would use their words to lift you up, offering comments like "Isn't she precious!" or "Look at how little she is; she's so cute!"

Now just to remind you, my sister is of Korean descent. There is no doubt that she is Asian. As adults, she and I decided to do a DNA test to see where our ancestors lived. My results show that my ancestors were scattered throughout the U.K. and Ireland, whereas Melyssa's ancestors were 100% Korean. We laughed when she received her results. There hadn't been much doubt about her origins. But you never know, right? At any rate, I bring this up because it played a role in the conversations that my mother's family had with her.

Instead of telling my parents how cute my sister was, Mom's siblings made comments such as, "Why did you adopt a baby from over there? Those kids are dirty" and "Those kids have diseases. We don't want that around here." When I first learned about those comments I was stunned. I was an adult when I first heard what had happened, but it still left me speechless. Feelings of anger, shock, and embarrassment washed over me. Then I wanted to know who had made the comments and why they had done so.

The comments started with two of my uncles. The "why" became a little more clear when I learned that one of them had served in the military during the Korean War. As a result of his wartime experience, he apparently hated Koreans. I cannot begin to guess what he, or some of the soldiers who served with him, may have faced in combat. Wars produce violence and loss of life, so I am sure that his wartime experiences had a negative impact. As awful as that may have been, it had no tie to the beautiful infant that my parents now held in their arms. My uncle had no excuse for spewing hateful comments while his sister held the child that she had welcomed into her family.

The term used to describe people who hold negative views of people from other cultures is "xenophobic." Essentially this means they have a dislike or prejudice against people from other countries. Members of my mother's family held xenophobic views of Koreans, and they were vocal in expressing them. They spoke loudly, and their words ended up influencing the family around them. I don't understand it, nor can I get my head around the fact that these comments were tolerated. No one pushed back, even though resistance is a typical reaction when a loud-mouthed bully holds center court. I would be lying if I said that I haven't thought long and hard about traveling to where one of my uncles currently lives so that I could confront him face to face about his hurtful comments.

When I thought about doing this, however, I realized it would serve no useful purpose other than allowing me to satisfy an angry impulse. My uncle doesn't deserve a shred of my time or energy, so let's move on.

In any event, the conversations that took place between my parents and my mother's family created the first cracks in the foundation of my mother's mental state and in my parents' relationship with my mother's family. To take it further, the negative reactions also began to damage Earl and Beth's marriage.

It is common to think of the damage that a physical altercation might have on people during a fight. A physical fight can potentially cause injuries such as bruising, cuts, or worse. Physical wounds typically heal with time, however, while hurtful words continue to bring pain long after they have been inflicted. When they come from a loved one, they stay even longer, and the pain can be even greater. The hurtful words that were said by my mother's family hurt her deeply and also planted a seed of doubt. The pain that was inflicted would grow over time within my mother. Those conversations also pushed my dad to stay away from my mother's family for quite a while. Whenever possible, he would avoid going to their homes just to steer clear of potential confrontations. Instead, he and my mother tried to deal with these comments internally. This would contribute to some of the arguments that were starting to take place between them. With family get-togethers being a common occurrence for my mother's family, how were they going to deal with the negative remarks? Would they avoid going, or would they go anyway, knowing that some family members would be watching them with hostility?

The conversations between my mother and her family left a mark and were the beginning of a series of events that would weigh on her mind and loosen her grip on her roles as a mother and a wife. An avalanche can start with one small disturbance at the top of a mountain and then acquire momentum, ultimately building up into a crushing amount of force that can destroy everything in its path. These early arguments were the beginning of a personal avalanche for our family.

P

EARLY TROUBLE

My father was an auto mechanic for many years, and the hours he worked were very consistent: Monday through Saturday from 8 to 5, creating a predictable weekly routine within our home. My mother stayed home for several years when my sister and I were young, which provided a stable schedule for our days as well. We had breakfast every morning and were busy playing with our toys soon after. Melyssa was crawling at this point, and the two of us enjoyed exploring anything we could find.

One day my dad broke the daily routine. For some reason, he finished work early that day and headed home. When he arrived at our house, he walked in and proceeded to change from his work uniform into his casual clothes. As he did, he heard Melyssa crying in her crib. The crying persisted, so he went into her room to check on her. When a small child is crying, it typically means they are hungry, tired, needing a diaper change, or hurt in some way. He couldn't figure out what the issue was, so he called out to my mother. She came in, and he asked her what she thought Melyssa needed. She told him that my sister had fallen while playing and began crying due to the fall. She went on to say that she couldn't stop Melyssa from crying, so she put her in her crib.

After looking her over and trying to calm Melyssa with no success, my parents took her to a doctor to be examined. She continued to cry the entire time that it took to drive to the doctor's office. After examining her, the doctor concluded that her shoulder had been dislocated. Luckily, he was able to pop it back into the socket and give her something for the pain. Melyssa calmed down, and we were able to go back home.

The incident didn't end there, though. It triggered a follow-up visit from a representative of DHHS (Department of Health and Human Services) who came to our house a day later to investigate what had happened. My parents had to answer several questions to provide exact details about their involvement.

Since my mother had been the only adult who was at home when Melyssa was injured, she took the brunt of the questions. She repeated the same explanation that she had given my father earlier: that my sister had fallen down and begun to cry. On the surface, that explanation may sound plausible. In theory, a child could be active and stumble while playing, which could cause them to dislocate their shoulder. There are many variables that would need to happen for this to occur, but it is within the realm of possibility.

The trouble with Mom's explanation is that the likelihood of a dislocated shoulder happening to a child who is walking, running, and jumping is plausible, but the odds of it happening to a child who is learning to crawl are slim to none. Melyssa was learning to crawl at this stage of her life. That fact focused attention squarely on my mother. The visit to the doctor and the follow-up from DHHS were troubling, to say the least. It cast doubt and started to undermine the trust between my parents.

Many years later, my father would share stunning details about that day. After some time had passed, he had asked my mother more questions about what had happened. It didn't make sense to him, and he was trying to settle things in his mind. The tension between my parents surrounding the incident had continued to be an issue, and he had hoped that by talking it through one more time he could put it to rest. He was able to break through and get Mom to open up a bit. As she started to talk, her story changed. Melyssa had been playing that day, and something had occurred that caused her to cry. In the scheme of things this would be a normal daily occurrence that any parent with a toddler would encounter. Was she hungry? Did she fall and bump herself? Was she crying because she wanted something? The answer is unknown.

My mother went on to say that she had picked Melyssa up and tried to console her. Holding her wasn't helping, and Mom began to grow agitated as the crying persisted. She then admitted that in a fit of frustration, she had shaken my sister. She told Dad that she "shook her so hard thinking something would happen." The shaking made my sister cry even more, which led my mother to place her in her crib.

This admission mortified my father. What exactly had Mom wanted to happen? What had led her to become so frustrated that she reached a level where physically shaking Melyssa was how she reacted? Did she truly shake her, or did she grab her arm, resulting in the dislocation? Those unanswered questions led to more doubt. More importantly, the doubt led to a very big question: how could the family move forward while knowing this had happened?

P

UNRAVELING A ROPE

A rope can be a strong tool that can be used in endless ways: to bind things together, to pull or secure an object, or to connect something. A rope is made up of individual strands that are twisted or braided together to add strength. After heavy use over time, some of the outer strands may get nicked or frayed. Depending on how badly the strand is damaged, it might stay intact or it may separate. When the fibers begin to separate, the rope loses some of its strength. If you continue to damage each of the strands, you will eventually expose the center strand. Once the center strand breaks, the rope is useless.

If I use the analogy of the strands being the faith that we lean on, relationships we have, or strong feelings we have built up, then you can see how easily the strands can be broken throughout our lives. Our rope can be strengthened or broken quickly. For my mother, one of the first strands to fray had been her relationships with her siblings. Their hurtful comments about Melyssa had damaged that strand quickly. Those conversations were the beginning of the unraveling of Mom's rope. The shaking incident frayed another strand. Once the unraveling started, it was very difficult to prevent the fraying from continuing.

In some cases, you can repair your rope. You can see a therapist, talk to someone within your church such as a priest or pastor, or speak with family members or friends. Each of those conversations present the opportunity to heal and to strengthen your rope. For my mother, her attempt to repair her rope started with a conversation with a pastor in our church. I remember one of those conversations very clearly. Again, I was a child so I couldn't comprehend everything that was being said, but I could pick up on the emotions involved. I was playing on one side of our living room while my parents spoke with our pastor on the other side. I was young enough that they weren't concerned about me hearing what they said. They knew that the meaning of their words would not register with me.

For some reason I can still visualize the scene. My parents sat on the couch while the pastor sat in a chair. The pastor asked questions, and my mother and father quietly answered them. My mother cried at times, and this stuck with me. The tone of the conversation was serious. Later in life, I came to understand that those conversations with our pastor were meant to support and uplift my parents. They were meant to strengthen the strand of the rope that represented their faith. The church was where friends who had also adopted children had led my parents to the adoption agency. So now, when they were having difficulty with my sister, they were again turning to the church to find support. Their faith would help them in the short term, but ultimately that strand would fray even more and eventually break.

Melyssa and Patrick hanging on the couch. Melyssa was 4 months old here. 1973.

One of our first family photos. Earl and Beth holding Patrick and Melyssa,1973.

Look at those smiles! Patrick and Melyssa ready
for the photo to be taken. 1974.

Front steps of our house. 1974.

Family photo at our house, 1976.

$\mathcal{P}$

GROWING TOGETHER
AND A NEW ADDITION

I have tried to scour my mind to remember as much as possible about those early years, but the only reliable memories I have during this time are of the family members and friends that we were around the most. Some of the toys and games that I played with during these early years stand out as well, of course!

We had a lot of fun playing and laughing during the next few years, for sure.

Now that Melyssa was getting a little bit older, we were able to do more together. Having friends in the neighborhood added to the fun as well.

Daily Big Wheel races down the sidewalk were common, in addition to swinging on our backyard playset. Playing with building blocks or engaging in never-ending games of hide-and-seek were always in the mix as well.

Holidays were celebrated with all of the excitement that you would expect. The family felt tight and loving. To me, life was good during this time of our lives. My mother and father shared every duty in the household and made sure we had fun and were attended to. My parents focused on keeping things centered on Melyssa and me, and that helped them to reduce any tension.

Things were rolling along until a surprise dropped in our laps. My mother was pregnant! It was more of a surprise to my parents, who had truly thought they would not be able to have another child. They suddenly had to change their perspective on what our family looked like and what our future would be. Adding another family member meant reconsidering the house we lived in and figuring out how they would approach work and our regular daily routines. Mentally, it was also a shift, as my mother had thought she was unable to give birth to another child. This had been my parents' motivation for adopting Melyssa, and now my mother was pregnant and coming to terms with the fact that she was actually going to have another child.

I was four years old when the pregnancy came to light and five years old when my second sister arrived on the scene. My sister Dereith (Dere for short) arrived in the middle of 1975. Our family of five was off and running with an infant, a 2½-year-old, and a five-year-old. With the new addition, the close feeling within the household continued to remain strong. From my perspective, life was even better now that I had another sibling to play with. As far as I knew, I had everything I could have wanted at that point in my life. No complaints from this five-year-old! We had a full house, and it seemed like I was going to have even more fun than before!

P

BRUISES

Kids get bruises all the time. When you are a child, play is serious business! You are busy climbing, jumping, and getting into all sorts of mischief. Each of those activities can find you tumbling down unexpectedly with a simple loss of balance. As children, we are almost fearless when it comes to some of our physical adventures. With those tumbles, children may end up with a bruise more often than not. Their legs and arms seem to take the hits the most. While it is common to see a bruise in those spots, it is not as common to see bruises on the lower back or buttocks. If they do show up in those areas, observers might question the type of fall that had caused bruises to show up on that part of the body.

As a toddler and young child, Melyssa had what appeared to be bruises on her body, primarily on her lower back and buttocks. My parents noticed them but didn't think too much of them as they were faint at first. They had been the only ones with her and knew that no physical harm had been done. She had not fallen, nor had anything happened that would have caused these random marks. As young parents they were still figuring out many things about raising children, and this was a new one. Melyssa wasn't upset, and the bruises didn't cause pain when anyone touched them. They would appear and then slowly subside over time. This appeared to be some sort of change that was part of Melyssa's growth. My parents grew accustomed to seeing them appear and disappear. However, for neighbors who babysat us, or teachers at school who saw us on a daily basis, their perception became a different reality. They noticed the "bruising" as well. Some of the marks were faint, while others appeared darker. When Melyssa needed help using the restroom or her shirt came up slightly, these adults jumped to a completely different conclusion about how the marks got there. Their initial reaction was to assume that the bruises had been caused by Melyssa being struck. My parents were the sole caregivers, and in the eyes of bystanders they were the ones who took care of Melyssa and the only ones who could have inflicted the bruising. Neighbors and teachers began to talk, and once again my parents were being questioned.

My mother began to worry. Not only were trusted neighbors talking about our family, but teachers at the school where she had recently begun to work were talking as well. This talk led to my parents being questioned about Melyssa's safety and well-being.

My mother's friends and coworkers were now assuming that she had hurt her child. The thought of this worried her immensely and took a toll on her mentally. Another strand of my mother's rope was beginning to fray.

My dad took Melyssa to the doctor to have the marks examined. This time the diagnosis produced a different type of shock for my parents. The doctor told them that the spots were not bruises at all. They were "Mongolian spots," a type of birthmark caused by pigment in the skin. The medical term for this is "congenital dermal melanocytosis." The spots occur when some of the skin's pigment gets trapped in the deeper layers of skin during a child's development. When the pigment does not reach the surface, it appears as a gray, greenish, blue, or black mark. Some infants are more likely to get them than others. They are particularly common in children with darker skin, such as those of Asian, Hispanic, Native American, and East Indian descent. They typically occur on the back or buttocks. They resemble bruises but do not cause pain and are not the result of an injury. Most infants or toddlers will outgrow them, and the spots will disappear.

The doctor informed my dad that Melyssa was healthy and that the spots had not been caused by physical injury. It was a relief to both of my parents to hear the news, because it would clear everything up. In some ways it did. However, even though there was an explanation for the spots, it couldn't erase the belief in my mother's mind that people around her had formed different conclusions. Her anxiety over this would be added to the list of things weighing her down mentally. All of her apprehension centered on Melyssa, and the list was growing.

P
FILLING THE DAUGHTER ROLE

Now that our family had grown, my parents saw the need for a more spacious home. Dere was now two, Melyssa was five, and I was eight. Our house was a busy place as we brought our toys out and played on any given day. To add space, our parents decided to build a new house in a subdivision that was in the early stages of development. They would build a home from the ground up, giving all of us a fresh start. The new house was only a mile from where we currently lived, so it was easy to keep tabs on it as construction was underway.

Preparing to move into a new home was exciting and gave my parents a boost of energy. There are many fun decisions to make when you build a new home! These include paint choices, carpet swatches, and thoughts about where you will place all of your furniture. Building a new house gave our family an opportunity to focus on something new, and for my mother it was a welcome distraction from the trouble she was having. Another positive point was that the new house was so close to where we were currently living that there would be no need to change schools. Our normal routines would stay the same.

The impending move provided a distraction for my mother, but it didn't take away the feelings she was struggling with. She continued to have challenges involving how she dealt with Melyssa. Dere was a toddler, which meant she needed more attention. At that point my mother focused on Dere as well as the new house. As she did, her love for Dere grew and one thing became increasingly apparent: Dere filled a daughter role that my mother had struggled to find with Melyssa. As my mother focused her attention and affection on Dere, she distanced herself from Melyssa. My mother was struggling to show the same type of affection toward Melyssa as she did to Dere. The discomfort associated with the disconnection continued to build as each day passed. My mother began to recognize how she felt, but she didn't know how to deal with it as she had had no outlet. Instead, the feelings stayed bottled up, ultimately affecting her mood as the days went on.

Conversations with our pastor helped, but they didn't change the fact that Mom's resentment was continuing to grow. It was beginning to snowball. All of the hurtful events that had occurred since Melyssa came into our lives were adding weight to the snowball as it rolled down the hill. My father was able to fill the gap between my mother and Melyssa to a certain degree. As much as he tried to smooth things over, however, the gap still existed. As time passed, the gap was widening, and there were limits to what he could do.

$\mathcal{P}$
TRIAL RUN

We moved into our new house in December of 1979, which meant that the holidays became even more exciting. We were in a new home at Christmas, and out of school, too! Melyssa and I had a blast building a snow fort and then holding epic snowball fights. When it was too cold to go outside, we filled our time putting puzzles together and watching TV. We always found things to do together, and the days and nights of our break from school were filled with fun. The break ended sooner than we wished, and it was time to head back to school again. Melyssa was in first grade and I was in third, and we were excited to get back into the groove with school.

Our new home and the familiar routine of school improved the outlook of my parents, but it didn't erase their underlying anxiety. My mother continued to struggle with her feelings toward Melyssa. It was growing more apparent that my father couldn't fill the gap that existed as he tried to make sure that we were receiving the attention that we needed. My parents continued to have strained conversations, and I sensed that trouble was brewing. Their conversations were serious and held behind closed doors most of the time. The times that I was able to hear any part of the discussion made me realize they were discussing Melyssa and expressing how they felt. My father continued to ask my mother what was happening and why she felt so disconnected. My mother continued to answer with a simple, "I don't know." The conversations always seemed to end in frustration. As the talks continued, Mom and Dad started discussing the future and trying to find a solution. The solution they found came through talks with friends at their church. Through those friends, they met a couple that were willing to help.

A short 45-minute drive from Omaha into Iowa takes you to a town called Woodbine, and in that town lived the Hinze family. Jack and Jan Hinze, along with their four children, lived in a home nestled on a wooded plot of land just outside of town. They were mutual friends with several of my parents' church friends and were willing to bring Melyssa into their home temporarily as my parents tried to work through my mother's issues. To begin the process, our family visited my dad's parents who lived two hours from Omaha in a small town in Iowa. After a weekend visit, we started to make our way back home but stopped in Woodbine. I didn't think too much of it, as we were told that we were visiting friends of my parents. My parents talked with their friends, and we were introduced to their children. The kids were similar to us in age, so it made it easy to get to know them. They showed us around the land that they lived on, and we had fun walking through trails on their property for a few hours.

Before long it was time to get back in the car to finish our trip home. What I didn't realize was that Mom, Dad, Dere, and I were leaving, but Melyssa was staying. This was going to be her new temporary home. As our car pulled away from the Hinze family's home, I sat in disbelief. I felt scared. It didn't make sense, and I had zero control over what was happening. My parents made an excuse to keep me calm as we drove back home, but my mind started to spin with questions. What was happening? Why was Melyssa not coming home? How long would she stay with the Hinze family? I didn't know the answers to those questions, and I continued to repeat them in my mind as we drove home in silence.

Even though the drive home from Woodbine took less than an hour, the Hinze family lived far enough away to create the distance that my parents wanted. By having Melyssa stay with the Hinze family, my mother could address her feelings and see if "distance makes the heart grow fonder," as the saying goes. For Melyssa, it meant being in a home with four older children. Jack and Jan had six other children, and now Melyssa found herself as the youngest child in their group.

Before leaving Melyssa with Jack and Jan, my parents talked with them and made plans. The plans involved a visitation schedule that would have my father dropping by the Hinze household periodically and then making more frequent visits. After having no contact with us for a few weeks, Melyssa would begin making weekend visits. This meant Melyssa would eventually be coming back to our home on Saturday and Sundays. By having the distance during the week and then slowly integrating everyone together on the weekends, my parents thought my mother might be able to regain some control over her feelings.

This arrangement may have been designed to help my mother figure out where she stood with her thoughts and feelings, but it made me feel confused, anxious, and scared. My sister who I did everything with was now gone. I was told I would see her later. What did this mean? Why was this happening? If I did something wrong, would the same thing happen to me? Would each of us kids also have to go away and then visit our home on the weekends as a punishment? That was what it felt like to me as a kid.

If I was asking myself those questions, then what must Melyssa have been thinking? She was the one who had been removed. I would have been scared to death if I had been left with another family. I couldn't escape those thoughts, and it made me start to question my parents and everything that I thought they were supposed to be. The nice way to describe the situation would be to say it was "unsettling." Replace *unsettling* with "frightening" or "terrifying" and you would be more accurate. I was nine years old and my sister was seven. We were told what was happening, and we were not asked for our opinions.

We were suddenly split apart after a weekend visit with our grandparents and a quick stop at our parents' friends' house. I was told that Melyssa would "visit" us on the weekends. I didn't know what to think or whom to trust. The images I had of our family and the roles that my parents were supposed to play were suddenly falling apart. I had no outlet for my fear. I could only listen and observe what my parents were doing. As a child you are supposed to listen to your parents and trust in what they tell you. I was told that everything would be okay. Maybe so, but my best friend was gone, and it didn't feel like anything was going to be the same after that.

M

WOODBINE

My dad was from a small town in Iowa called Glidden, and as we were growing up we had a lot of fun visiting our grandparents in the home that he had grown up in. I will never forget the last visit I had there, though. I was in first grade, and we had spent the weekend visiting with relatives and playing. On our way back to Omaha, we stopped to visit some family friends. Well, at least I thought that was what we were doing. I remember Dad driving down a long gravel driveway, and at the end sat a big brown house. On the right-hand side of the property was a huge pasture as well as a dirt track for bicycles and motorcycles. There were trees everywhere, and it felt like we were in a forest depending on which direction we looked.

Patrick and I hopped out of the back seat and followed my parents to the house. We were greeted by a man, a woman, and several kids. I remember standing close to my brother and my dad as I took everything in. My parents introduced us to the couple, whose names were Jack and Jan Hinze. After that, they introduced us to the Hinze children: Shane, Chad, Jackie, Josh, Amber, and Jason. Jack and Jan had four biological children and had adopted two other children as well. I remember watching Patrick run off with the boys to the pasture to ride dirt bikes. I stood close to my dad because I still wasn't sure what this visit was about.

Jan took my mom, dad, and Dere inside while Jack asked me if I wanted to watch the kids ride dirt bikes. I nodded yes, and we walked into the pasture to watch the others. As we walked through the pasture and trees, I remember thinking how awesome the place was. There was so much space, and it was amazing that all of it was next to their house.

I'm not sure how long we were gone, but after a while Jack told me and a few of the other kids that we should head back to the house. As we got closer to their home, I realized that my parents' car was gone. As I looked around, I didn't see my parents or my brother and sister. I started to get scared and asked Jack where they were. He said, "Let's go into the house and we will talk."

We went in and sat down, and that is when I learned that my parents had not just stopped to visit with their friends on the spur of the moment. This visit had been intentional, and they had left me with this family. I remember feeling confused and starting to cry. As I looked down, I saw my luggage from the trip to visit my grandparents. It was now sitting in this unfamiliar house with me. The one thing that stuck in my head was that my parents had left me with my luggage and a brand-new bag of socks, which meant that they had planned ahead. It looked like I was going to be with the Hinze family for a while.

Jack and Jan were very nurturing and tried to comfort me as much as they could that night. All of the kids were also very kind to me, which helped as well. I ended up sharing a room with their daughter, Amber, who was the same age as I was. She was also Asian, which was comforting in a way. Amber showed me her toys, and it helped me take my mind off my parents for a while. I remember crying myself to sleep that night, and as I did, I kept telling myself that if I just went to sleep my family would be back in the morning.

I woke up the next morning and walked out of the bedroom to find Jan cooking breakfast, with all of the kids seated around the table. Everyone was sweet and made room for me so I could sit among them. I could barely eat as I kept thinking that at some point during the day my parents would come back to pick me up. Thinking about it lifted my spirits, and I started to feel better. Everyone finished their breakfast, and we all headed outside to play. It was fun because they had so much land to run around on! We went exploring in the woods and could run and play for hours. As the day shifted into night, I watched the clock and slowly realized that my family wasn't coming back to pick me up. Just like the first night, I cried myself to sleep and hoped they would come back for me the next day.

As the days went on, things got a little better as I continued to bond with the kids in the family. We continued to play well together, and this helped to keep my mind occupied and boosted my spirits. Things changed one day, though, as Jan had news for me. She pulled me aside and told me that my dad was coming to visit me that weekend. I couldn't believe it! I was so excited! The days couldn't pass quickly enough!

Saturday came, and I waited anxiously for my dad to arrive. I saw his car come down the long gravel driveway and I ran quickly to greet him. I felt like I would burst with excitement as he got out of the car with a big smile and hugged me. After a minute I remember asking him where my mom, Patrick, and Dere were. He told me that they had a lot of things to do and couldn't come. I accepted his explanation, shrugged, and said, "Okay" as I gave him a huge hug. I started telling him about what I had been up to. I told him how nice everyone was, and I asked him if he wanted to walk with me on some of the trails

I had been exploring. He said, "Sure," and we walked and continued to talk about the things that I had been doing.

We had so much fun as the day went on! As the day was winding down, I remember gathering my luggage so we could load it into the car and head back to our home. My dad looked at me and said, "You can't come home yet, but I will be back soon to see you again." I ran and held on to him as I began to cry. I kept asking him why I couldn't come home with him. He held me and just kept saying, "I will see you soon." Jan had to peel me off of my dad and continued to hold me as my dad walked to his car and then drove away. He had left again.

It was like this for months. Dad would come and visit me and then leave at the end of the day. The new routine was very difficult for me. I would work through my sadness during the week and get excited when he visited on the weekend, only to be crushed as I watched him leave me each time. It was a tough cycle, and the Hinze family did everything they could to boost me back up after each visit. The emotional highs and lows were difficult to deal with, though. I continued to live in limbo, and it hurt so much.

I often wondered what Patrick and Dere were doing but was fortunate to get sidetracked that summer by playing with the kids outdoors and at the community pool. Before long, summer ended and I started the school year in second grade at the same school the Hinze family attended. I was beginning a new routine yet again, and I started to wonder if this was how it would be forever. That thought changed one day when Jack and Jan told me I would be going back home for a visit. I was so excited! I couldn't believe that I was going back to my home.

As I looked forward to going home, I also started to feel sad because I thought I wouldn't see the Hinze family again. We had started to bond, and I had grown to feel a solid level of trust in them. It couldn't stop feeling excited, though, as

I anxiously waited for the weekend. I remember my dad coming to pick me up and then being filled with anticipation as I sat in the car on the way back to Omaha. I think I talked my dad's ear off during the entire trip! I couldn't wait to go home and see Patrick and Dere.

When we arrived, I ran into the house to see my siblings and my mom. They were so excited to see me and hugged me instantly. I remember feeling so happy at that moment! Saturday was a blur as we played all day and had fun laughing at everything. Sunday started the same way, and it felt like things were shifting back to normal. It was like we hadn't missed a beat with each other. That feeling quickly fell to pieces when the weekend was over and I was told that I was going back to the Hinze family.

It turned out that I was only home for a weekend visit. I couldn't believe it. When it was time for me to leave the house, my brother and I just stared at each other before I turned and walked out the door. We didn't know how to react. It felt like the energy was drained from us in that instant. I was silent as Dad drove me back to Iowa. It felt like a cruel trick had been played on me. How could they let me come back and have so much fun only to take me back on Sunday evening?

I felt like my world had collapsed, and it took me days to get back to normal. Jack and Jan had said this was a "visit," but it hadn't registered in my head when they said it. I had thought I was going home for good. The reality was crushing. I ended up going back and forth for a few more weekend visits, which continued my up-and-down emotional rollercoaster.

But then things finally changed. I was told that my next visit wasn't just a visit. I was actually going home for good! Jack and Jan told my parents that they needed to decide what they wanted to do. The Hinze family felt that my parents couldn't continue to do what they were doing to me. It felt like I was a yo-yo with emotional highs and lows, and the Hinze family had to pick up the pieces every time my hopes were crushed. The back-and-forth between homes was finally coming to an end, and it felt like I was finally going to find some peace. I could be with my family, sleep in my own bed again, and finally be where I belonged.

HOME AGAIN

As the holidays approached, my parents began to think that maybe the experiment could end. They began planning to bring Melyssa home for good. The Hinze family was supportive but hesitant, as they had grown to love Melyssa. In the end, they knew my parents had the right to bring her home, and that is what happened.

Melyssa came home and suddenly my life brightened up. I was reunited with my sister and my heart soared! The power of that bond was strong, and it lifted both of our spirits. My best friend was back, and it wasn't just for the weekend! Melyssa and I had made it through the rough patch, and we could be a family again. I could not have asked for a better Christmas gift. The winter break was a ton of fun, and when it ended we returned to school with a sense of optimism.

School was back in session, but due to the fact that our elementary school didn't offer a second-grade class (weird, I know), Melyssa had to take a bus to a different school for that grade. I had done the same thing the year before, so I knew exactly what it was like. I knew we would be in the same school the following year, so it wasn't a big deal.

Our mornings, afternoons, and evenings returned to a familiar routine. We made it through the end of winter and started to get ready for spring.

Ignorance is bliss, especially when you are a child. I had noticed that my parents were starting to become short-tempered with each other, but I didn't believe that it would lead to any trouble. It just sounded like bickering to me, so I didn't pay much attention. As it turned out, it did lead to more trouble.

I didn't want to believe that it would happen again, but my mother was starting to feel the same way she had felt before. She had thought Melyssa's time away meant that she would now be able to show Melyssa the same level of love and affection she showed me and Dere. Mom had hoped this would happen on its own, but in reality, it did not. She had never really dealt with the origins of her negative feelings. My mother had used time and distance away from Melyssa as a solution, rather than talking about her true feelings with my father or a counselor.

In the past, Mom had tried to talk to my father or their pastor from church, but now she was trying to keep her feelings bottled up. Out of sight, out of mind. But when Melyssa returned to the household, my mother had to face those feelings head on. She continued trying to push her feelings aside, which allowed her to project an image that things were okay to everyone around her. It kept our household calm, but Mom couldn't continue doing that for very long, and my father started to realize it. Tension grew between my parents as they realized that everything they had tried to fix was still in disarray. All of their attempts to fix the issue had failed. Their arguments were starting to become more frequent, and at the heart of them was one simple question: If nothing had worked before, what would happen now?

P ULTIMATUM

The tension and arguments between my parents continued as we rolled into spring. The conversations that took place in front of me and my sisters were short and lacked emotion. Their talks behind closed doors were louder and lasted much longer. One of them would finally leave the room they were in, slamming the door behind them.

My father tried to keep things calm for my sisters and me, but we could tell something was off. He did his best to keep things going. He would find time to play with us, or at least make sure we had things set up to play independently. That was important, as my mother had disconnected from us at this point. She wasn't showing Melyssa the same level of affection as she would show me or Dere, and now my father was addressing it. The plan to have Melyssa spend time away from the family hadn't worked. My mother didn't know what to do, so she put distance between herself and the rest of the family. To cope, she would retreat into music and books. We would often see her sitting in a chair in our living room listening to records and reading.

Mom loved reading Harlequin romance novels. She would trade bags of them with my aunt and my grandmother. She would put a record on the turntable, sit down with a book, and then she was to be left alone. With the music playing and a perfect romance unfolding on the pages in front of her, she could escape the troubling issues that she was battling. It was a pure escape for her, but it did nothing to help us at that moment. That pattern continued as the days passed.

The days of emotional distance turned into a few months. Spring was in view, and we knew that the school year would end soon and our summer break would be upon us. My parents realized that they had to do something, but their options were now limited. They had begun to discuss the situation with each side of their own families. After all of those discussions, one thing was apparent: my mother had made up her mind that Melyssa had to go.

A few options were on the table. Mom and Dad each had a sister who had offered to take Melyssa into their family and raise her. Both of our aunts were willing to take things on and had the means to do it. In theory, it sounded like a viable option to my parents. A trusted family member could take Melyssa in and raise her, and everyone would feel comforted knowing she was being raised within our extended family. That option was considered and then dismissed by my mother. It did not sit well with her. She did not want it to happen because from her vantage point it would mean the adoption had been a failure. How could she watch another family member happily raise the little girl that she had been unable to parent? Seeing that would eat at her, and she refused to do it.

My father had been going back and forth with all of this. He would have gone along with the option of a family member raising Melyssa because at least it would have meant that he could still be close to her. My mother wouldn't accept the idea, so it left only two options. He started to ask himself if he could raise Melyssa as a single father if he and my mother separated or got a divorce.

In the end, my mother quickly announced an ultimatum that proved to be too much for my father to take. She told him, "Your life will be tough if you take Melyssa." She then threatened him by saying, "You won't see your kids again (Dere and me) if you don't follow through with giving up Melyssa." He struggled with her ultimatum. It proved to be too much for my dad to bear, and he ultimately agreed to go along with her decision.

The outcome was devastating. Melyssa would be removed from our household and put into the foster system in the state of Nebraska. Eight years after she had been adopted by my parents as an infant, she would begin the adoption journey again.

P
LETTING GO

My father was tasked with picking up Melyssa at school and then dropping her off with someone from the state. She was about to enter the foster care system, but before that happened he would pick up Melyssa and then meet my mom. Dad drove to the school after arrangements had been made to release Melyssa early that day. My parents had used the excuse of a dental appointment to get her out of school.

Dad had some time to spare before he was supposed to meet my mom, so he decided to take Melyssa to a park. Melyssa loved playing on the swings and having fun on the playground. Time with her was running short, and wanted her to have some fun first. He knew that he was going to be late for the appointment, but he also knew these precious minutes were the final moments they would have together. After eight years of raising Melyssa from an infant to a young girl, he was going to hand his daughter over and say goodbye for the last time.

My father knew it was getting late and they needed to go, so he called Melyssa over and they walked back to the car. He later told me, "I hated that drive. Everything inside of me knew that I shouldn't be doing it, and yet I still did." I have tried to place myself in his shoes in the hope that I might be able to understand how he felt or to think through the options that he had. The truth is that I can't place myself there. I can't understand the situation, nor can I comprehend how my parents came to the decision to walk away. Now that I have become a parent, too, I still can't wrap my head around it.

If this were a movie, then this might have been the scene where my dad made the bold decision to turn the car around and drive back home. He could have stood his ground and fought back by putting the kids first. Instead, he felt defeated, and he drove on to meet my mom at her parents' house before meeting with a caseworker from the state. They met with my grandparents and a few aunts and uncles to let them have one final opportunity to see Melyssa. After that, they made the drive to the state office.

The part of this story that bothers me most is that Melyssa didn't know what was happening at this point. It wasn't until they reached the state office and started talking to the caseworker that things started to register with her. When she realized what this meeting meant, she started to cry and held onto my parents. They attempted to console her by telling her that things were going to be okay, and then the caseworker quietly signaled that they should leave. They walked out and drove away, believing that was the end of things. In reality, it was just the end of one portion of the story. They still had to tell me and Dere what had happened, and that was going to be another big hurdle.

Melyssa had been placed with a caseworker, but that wouldn't last long. She had been paired with a foster family and would be staying in their home that evening. In fact, the family she would be living with was in the Omaha area. They lived in Millard, which blended into the edge of the city and was only ten minutes from where we lived. We would never know that, though, since she was now in the foster system and information about Melyssa's whereabouts would be kept private. As an adult, I have driven many times through the area where Melyssa was living. I think about the fact that she was a quick drive away and yet we never ended up crossing paths. It hurts to know how close she really was. When I was a child, though, it felt like she might have been half a world away.

M

1981

I will never forget the day I was separated from my family. It started like any other normal day. Patrick and I got ready to go to school. Patrick was in fourth grade, I was in second grade, and our little sister wasn't in school yet. Patrick and I went to different schools due to our grade school separating certain grade levels.

We sat around the table eating our breakfast and watching *Captain Kangaroo*. Patrick was attending the school where my mom worked, but I had to catch a school bus to get to my school. The bus was about to come, and I gathered my things before heading out the door. I said goodbye to my brother and sister, not realizing that it would be the last time I ate breakfast with or spoke to them. I was excited for the day to begin, because Pinky the Elephant was going to visit my second-grade classroom later that afternoon. This was a big deal! Pinky was an elephant who talked about poison control.

The morning went quickly, and after lunch my teacher came up to me and told me to gather my things because my dad was here to get me. I was confused and disappointed because it meant I wouldn't be able to see Pinky the Elephant.

I gathered my belongings and walked down to the school office where I found my dad waiting. He signed me out, and we walked hand-in-hand to his car. I asked him where we were going and told him how sad I was about missing Pinky. He told me I had a dentist appointment. This was a surprise, but I just nodded and jumped into the car with my bag. I sat in the back seat and looked at the sky as we pulled away from the school. After a few minutes, my dad began to speak. He told me he loved me, and how I was so great. I just responded, "I love you, too!" He repeated it several times, and as he kept saying it, I started to think something was off. Normally he wouldn't repeat things several times.

We ended up driving to a park, so I thought it meant we had some extra time to play before the dental appointment. This was better than I had expected, and I quickly ran to the playground and jumped on the swings. I'm not sure how long we were there, because I was busy running around and laughing. This day was different, but it felt like I was getting to do something fun with my dad, so I didn't mind.

At a certain point my dad told me we had to go, so we walked over to the car and headed out once more. We drove for a while and then drove down a street that started to look familiar. As we pulled up, I realized we were turning into the driveway of my grandparents on my mom's side. As a family, we had spent a lot of time there. My brother and sister and I referred to our grandparents as Nan and Papa. A fun stop to see Nan and Papa made the day even better! It seemed odd since my dad had told me we were going to the dentist, but I wasn't complaining. It wasn't a dental exam, so it was great to me!

After the car came to a stop, I asked why we were there, and my dad said we just had to stop by for a minute. I didn't think anything of it as my dad grabbed my hand as we walked up to the house. We opened the door, and when we walked upstairs,

I saw that my mom was there along with my grandparents, my aunt, and an uncle. I now began to think something was going on, but I couldn't figure out what. They greeted me quietly as my dad had me sit down next to him. The silence in the room felt awkward. Anyone who spoke seemed to speak quietly, as if something bad had happened. That felt odd to me, as the family was usually loud and fun to be around. The conversation was very brief, and before I knew it, my parents and I were getting up to leave. Each of the family members smiled weakly as we said our goodbyes. I gave each of them a hug, and then we walked out to the car. I just assumed we had been picking up my mom and we would all go to the dentist together.

We drove for a bit and then pulled up to a building I didn't recognize. We walked into the building and were greeted by a man who led us into an office. I immediately knew I wasn't seeing the dentist that day. As my parents spoke to me, I heard the words that no child ever wants to hear: "Things aren't working out at the house, so you are going to go live with another family." I instantly started crying and hugged my dad. My mom and dad both had tears in their eyes. I remember holding onto my dad for dear life when a woman came in and told me to come with her. I couldn't let go of him as he said again, "Everything will be okay." I then unhooked my arms and walked into another room with her, and that was the last time I saw my mom and dad.

I remember crying as the woman held me in her arms and wiped my tears away. I soon would understand that this woman worked for the Nebraska Children's Home and would be placing me with a family. Prudy was her name, and she had been assigned as my caseworker. My relationship with Prudy was just beginning, and little did I know it would be a friendship that would last for a very long time.

P

1981

When you're a ten-year-old, getting out of school early to be with your dad seems like a pretty cool deal. I remember walking out of school that day and staring up at the sky as we walked to the car. I don't know why that sticks out, but for some reason I can remember the moment clearly. The sun was shining, the sky was blue, and no clouds were in sight.

I think the moment stuck out because the day felt different. It wasn't normal for me to get out of school early. It seemed like it must have been a special occasion. It's strange how random details stick out like that.

The ride home was quiet. My dad didn't say much other than to tell me that we would talk about why I was getting out of school when we got home. It was a short drive, so waiting to find out wasn't a big deal. We walked into the house, and I put down my backpack. I can picture the living room vividly. The memory is similar to recalling a scene from a film. You can remember where each of the characters were and how they interacted. But the mood was what sticks out the most in my memory. My parents' faces were somber. The tone when they spoke was calm and quiet. The group that was gathered consisted of my mother, father, younger sister Dere (who was five), and me. One key person was missing: my middle sister, Melyssa, who was eight at this point. She hadn't been pulled from school to come home and join this conversation. That seemed odd but was quickly explained. As my mother and father spoke to the two of us, things started to get confusing. Their words just didn't make sense to me. I mean, I heard what they were saying, but it didn't seem possible. The situation that they were describing was mind-blowing. It didn't take long to understand the reason behind this meeting, nor did it take long to understand what was happening:

- My sister Melyssa was leaving us, and she wasn't coming back.
- At that point, it had already happened.
- She was gone, along with all of her belongings.

I don't remember asking a lot of questions. At the age of ten you are capable of asking questions about random subjects all day long, but in this conversation my voice was gone. I could muster only a few.

My parents tried to justify what had happened and reassure us with a few key phrases:

- "Things have been very tough for Melyssa and Mom."
- "I know this is hard to understand."
- "She will be happier, and so will your mom."
- "It will help her."
- "It will help all of us."

I kept thinking "In what way?" I didn't know we needed that much help!

I remember the silence afterward. A phrase often used is "all the air was sucked out of the room." In this case, it certainly felt that way. Silence hung in the air, and it felt like time stood still.

I was in a daze as I walked to my bedroom and stretched out on the bed. I was trying to process what was happening. Normally I would have heard Melyssa playing in the room next to mine. Now our bedrooms were quiet. The entire house was silent.

Thoughts and questions swirled in my mind.

- What was happening?
- What did this mean?
- How could things have shifted so quickly?

Nothing had seemed different that morning. Melyssa and I had left for school together. It had started out as a normal day by all accounts.

The differences between my day and Melyssa's day started to stick out now.

My day had gone like this:

I had gotten out of school early so we could sit down and discuss what was happening. I was at home. I would have dinner that night as usual, and then the next day I would be back in school.

Melyssa's day had been completely different:

She had gotten out of school early but had not come home. What was her discussion like? Where was she having dinner that night? Where was she going to sleep that night? Would she be in a different school the next day? Finally, where was she going to live from now on?

Fear crept over me—a feeling that would last for many years. I would often wonder, "Am I next? Is Dere next?"

Melyssa had been temporarily removed before and had been able to come back. This time, my parents told us she would never be coming back.

If I or Dere did something wrong, would we suddenly be removed from the house forever, too?

What had Melyssa done that was so bad that my parents had decided to get rid of her?

These questions would play out in my head over and over for a long time to come.

From that day forward, I noticed subtle changes within the house. For example, three separate photo collage frames had been hanging in the hallway on the second floor. To walk downstairs, you had to go past them. My sisters and I each had our own collage. The frames held a collection of photos taken at various points of our childhood. They were fun to look at as we recalled the great memories captured in each photo. I'm a "counter." I will count objects and develop a pattern. Walking past the frames was a daily ritual. "One, two, three…" As I prepared to run down the stairs and go to school the next morning, my pattern was suddenly broken. "One, two…" I stopped in my tracks and stared at the wall. The three frames had silently shrunk down to two.

Melyssa's frame was gone.

Nothing was said.

It just happened overnight and suddenly became our new normal. Melyssa's absence hit me hard as I took it in. Her clothes, toys, and photos were gone. Every item with a memory of Melyssa attached to it had been taken away. We had no choice but to silently move forward. The memories in my head were now all I had to cling to, and I held onto them dearly.

M

MILLARD

I remember being held by Prudy as she rocked me and told me things were going to be okay. We sat together long enough for me to finally calm down. My tears were still flowing, but she wiped them away, gave me a hug, and helped me stand up. Prudy had a very strong voice, which caught me off guard and scared me a little. She didn't have a soft tone, but her gentle touch and hugs said more to me than her words did, and I could tell that she cared. Even with her calming reassurance, I was still nervous as I stood in this strange office and wondered what was going to happen next.

Prudy and I soon walked outside to her car. She explained that she was taking me to a nice family that would take care of me. Don and Shirley Unrau were their names, and they had two boys, Justin, who was five, and Ryan, who was two. They lived in Millard, which was on the edge of Omaha.

As she continued talking, I started to cry. All I wanted was to be back home with my parents and Patrick and Dere. Why was this happening? I soon felt angry with Prudy. I was blaming her for taking me to this family that I didn't want to be with.

I already had a family and now all of a sudden I didn't? It was just over?

My anger kept rising as I started to tell her I wasn't going to talk to them. I raised my voice and told her I didn't like them and that she needed to take me back to my mom and dad.

She said she couldn't take me back and continued to drive as she talked more about the new family. As she spoke, I blocked out her words as much as I could and continued to cry.

We soon turned into a nice housing development and then pulled into the driveway of my new home.

Prudy opened the back door of her car, and I slowly got out and walked with her against my will. She rang the doorbell, and a very slender, nicely dressed woman answered the door. She greeted us and brought us into the house where we were also greeted by a tall, blond man holding a small child that looked Hispanic and a young Asian boy. Prudy introduced me to everyone and then we all sat down in the living room. As we looked around the house, it seemed like everything was very put together and in its proper place. Everything looked very clean and uncluttered, as if there were no kids living there. That seemed strange at first, because I was used to playing and having kids with toys all around me. As the conversation continued, the Unraus began to tell me about their boys and then about themselves.

Don worked at a large construction company called Kiewit, and Shirley was a teacher.

Don traveled a lot, and in his free time he played racquetball and liked to run.

They were very calm, and when Shirley spoke she seemed very prim and proper with her answers.

After talking for a while, Prudy got up and said it was time for her to go and that she would come back very soon to see how things were going.

I started to panic and began to cry. I was being left in a strange new house again and the one person with whom I had formed a small connection was leaving. Shirley quickly took my hand and led me into the kitchen with Justin, the five-year-old, following us. She asked if I liked chocolate cookies, and I just shrugged to give her a "yes." We then began to bake cookies. It helped me get my mind off being left behind by Prudy.

After we finished baking the cookies, Shirley showed me my new bedroom. It was very nice, and the walls had been painted blue with pink flowers. It felt very girly and at the time slightly strange as I hadn't had my own room in a few years. We started to unpack my clothes, and that's when things started to feel very real for me. I suddenly realized that I was never going to see Patrick, Dere, or my mom and dad ever again. I started to cry and felt very alone.

Shirley calmly talked to me and tried to make me feel better, but it didn't help. We finished putting my clothes away, and as we did I was suddenly surprised. I couldn't believe it, but my parents had packed a small stuffed animal that had been one of my favorites. It was a pink cat that my aunt Kate had given me. At least I had something that reminded me of them.

Shirley told me she was going to make dinner, and she went downstairs. I remember lying on my new bed and crying as I hugged my pink cat, wondering what Patrick was doing and whether he missed me. I also wondered what the Hinze kids were doing, as they also had become a big part of my life. I wondered if any of them missed me or if I was someone who could easily be forgotten. Was I out of sight, out of mind to everyone? It all hurt as I thought about everything that had happened.

Don came into my room and told me it was time for dinner. I slowly got up and followed him, but I was afraid to tell him I wasn't hungry.

I can't recall what was for dinner, but I remember staring around the room in disbelief. I was sitting with yet another family for dinner, and it didn't seem real.

After dinner I helped clear the table and load the dishwasher and then everyone watched TV. I felt drained that night, yet somehow I was able to fall asleep.

Saturday morning came and I remember sitting in my bed and wondering if it was okay to go downstairs and watch cartoons. Patrick and I watched cartoons every Saturday like clockwork. We poured ourselves our own cereal without any adult supervision and then plopped down to watch our favorite cartoons. That was the best!

I decided to go downstairs and found that Justin was already watching cartoons. Shirley and Don were both up. Shirley poured me some cereal and told me that when I finished, she was going to introduce me to the next-door neighbors. They were the Mackeys, and their daughter Kristen was my age.

We walked over, and after the introductions Kristen and I quickly hit it off. We played all afternoon until I got called in for dinner. It was a good step forward and finally turned my attention to something fun.

After dinner, I was told that the next morning was Sunday and we would be going to church. I quickly found out that attending church was a big part of the Unraus' family life. The next morning at church I was introduced to so many people! I didn't feel comfortable being the center of attention, but I could tell the Unraus felt proud as they introduced me to their friends.

The week went by quickly, and I felt myself slowly adjusting to my new life. On Saturday, Shirley held a "welcoming shower" for me. All of her friends attended and brought gifts for me. I was excited to get new things, but in the back of my mind I felt like they were just replacing what I had already had. It made me think of my family. It reminded me of the toys Patrick and I used to play with. At that moment, I realized that I would never see Patrick again. I felt sad and alone, even with so many people around me.

Days went by, and then weeks, followed by months. I was adjusting to life with the Unraus. It was becoming my new normal.

Prudy stopped by for a visit, and things seemed to be going along smoothly. I saw her one or two times, and then she stopped coming around.

My new life brought new activities that helped to fill the time.

I was introduced to soccer and absolutely loved it! I took piano lessons, which seemed fun until I had to practice daily, which soon felt like a drag.

I became great friends with Kristen, and we became inseparable. We played outside as much as we could. We rode our bikes in our neighborhood, we were on the same soccer team, and that summer we had a lot of sleepovers. On hot days, we walked down to the Goodrich ice cream store and laughed as our cones dripped all over.

I was finally starting to feel happy, but it came with a condition that I set for myself: I was never going to love or let anyone get close to me. When I did, things never seemed to work out. The "family" that had been close to me couldn't seem to love me enough to keep me. I often asked myself why this had happened. What had I done? With my rule in place, I was trying to protect myself from being hurt again.

Summer was ending, and the new school year was about to begin. As I started third grade, I made several new friends at school. Some of my friends also attended our church, which made things even easier.

Going to a new school was a hard adjustment for me, and I struggled when it came to taking tests. I remember a particular time when I wasn't prepared for a test and decided to cheat. Well, that didn't go very well for me, and sure enough I got caught! Don and Shirley were so upset with me. Looking back, that was really the beginning of the end of my time with the Unraus. It wasn't that I couldn't do well with tests. That was just a reaction to how I was dealing with things. I had been having fun with friends and getting along with my new family, but my behavior was just masking what I was really feeling inside. At that point I didn't care anymore. I felt like I was just "there." I felt emotionless and sad on the inside most of the time. As I watched Don and Shirley, it seemed like they doted on the boys all the time. I didn't feel that I was "good enough." I didn't sit straight enough at the table, I wasn't smart enough to pass tests at school, or I wasn't proper enough. I decided that I wasn't the daughter they thought they were getting, so I shut down. I talked less. I felt deep down they were probably going to "get rid" of me just like the others had. I didn't make life easy for them, and I didn't really care.

We never really bonded, and I felt like I was just there to show off that they had a daughter. I always looked the part and was dressed nicely with my hair in place. But I didn't feel as if I truly belonged.

I don't recall having a close relationship with the boys. Ryan was so little, and Justin and I got along just fine, but nothing more. They were younger and not on the same level with me.

My behavior and attitude continued to shift, and things continued to feel like we were growing apart.

Finally, the day came. It was a weekday morning in the summer, and Don had left for work already. Shirley came into my room and started packing my things. She then proceeded to tell me that Prudy was on her way over to get me, and I was going to join another family. I didn't see Shirley shed a tear as she spoke matter-of-factly while continuing to pack my bag. I remember being shocked and then sad, but ultimately not surprised.

Prudy showed up, and we put my things in her car and were on our way.

I remember crying as we drove along. Here I was, again, in the back of Prudy's car, and I didn't know where my next stop was going to be.

At that point I didn't like Prudy very much because she was always the bearer of bad news. When she showed up, it meant I was leaving again.

She told me I was joining a family with three other girls in Bellevue. I couldn't have cared less. I just looked out the window and didn't say a word. I wished I could just be in a home where I could stay and not move again.

I should have been careful what I wished for.

$\mathcal{P}$

SO NOW WHAT?

Somehow, the daily routines in our family continued after Melyssa left. Things felt off, though. They were different. How could they not be? Of course, everything around me was the same: our house, my school, our mealtimes, basically everything I was accustomed to. My parents acted "normal" as they interacted with me and Dere. Being around extended family, teachers, and friends looked the same. Everyone tried to carry on in a normal state. But it wasn't normal. Not at all.

Looking back, it seems like something you would see on a TV show like the *Twilight Zone*. The plot of the episode would go like this: Something major happened. A life-changing event occurred within our family. In any normal universe, this event would shake any person or family to their core. Nothing would be the same.

It literally felt like a death in the family. After eight years, my sister was gone. Since her infancy we had been best friends. She was my closest companion.

Melyssa had been removed from our family, our extended family, our circle of friends, and from anyone we had known.

HOW COULD ANYONE PRETEND ANY OF THIS WAS NORMAL?

How could we move on the very next day, the next week, or the next month with this huge hole in our lives? Family or friends would interact with smiles and carry on conversations as if nothing out of the ordinary had happened. I remember so many times when I was walking around in a slight daze. I was in places that I was accustomed to like my house or school, where I had normally felt comfortable. I knew where I was and where things were supposed to be in those spaces. I would walk through them, and even though I had been in that space hundreds of times, it felt foreign. It felt unsettling. Something was missing. I wasn't complete. I felt nervous. Most of all, I felt vulnerable. Could the same thing happen to me? Could I be taken away, too? I started to question things and wonder what I could do to make sure I was good enough that there would be no reason for my parents to remove me, too. I looked to my parents for any sign of emotion. I wanted to see if they were upset about Melyssa being gone. I wanted to see if they would close ranks and draw us in closer.

Instead, I saw life continue as if nothing had happened. How could my parents not show that they were upset? Were they? Surely they were, because one of their children was gone, right? They were supposed to protect us with their lives. If you are a parent and something happened to one of your children, surely you would be distraught. But we saw no sign of that. We carried on like normal, and that was their way of trying to make us feel safe. They thought that if our routines were undisturbed, then we would stay calm and there wouldn't be any issues. They held onto this idea, and we had no choice but to move forward in a similar fashion. It was a terrible plan that would have lasting effects.

M

A CHANGE ONCE AGAIN

The drive from the Unraus' house to my new home felt long. I stared out the window at the sky and wondered where this trip would take me. In reality, the distance wasn't far as we went from Millard to Bellevue, which is another suburb of Omaha. Once again, I was on the edge of the city where I had spent most of my life. So close, and yet so far away. Prudy tried to talk with me, but I wouldn't really engage with her. The familiar routine of riding in her car to a new house wasn't a good feeling, so riding in silence seemed to fit.

We finally turned into a neighborhood and drove up a hill leading us to a well-kept house that sat on a corner.

Prudy and I walked to the front door, and the first person to greet us was a man who introduced himself as Gary Fliehmann. He was a short, middle-aged man who wore glasses and had a sparse amount of hair sticking out on his head. His wife Norma came out and quickly introduced herself next. She was slender, had gray hair, and spoke with a British accent. Her accent was interesting to me, and it made me wonder about their family. Upon first glance, she seemed old to me because of her gray hair. The women in my other families had been younger.

We walked into the house and sat down in the living room as Prudy began introducing me. There were other kids in the house, and as we were talking three girls filed in. I had assumed this was a foster home, so I wondered if I would meet other kids with different ethnic backgrounds like mine. As I scanned their faces, I discovered that my guess was partially right. Ruth was the oldest and in high school. She had a heavier build and looked to be of a mixed nationality. Next in line was Janet, who was very slender and looked to be in middle school. She had light skin, and I had no idea about her nationality. Finally came Sarah, who had long brown braids and appeared to be of Indian or Hispanic descent. She was the same age as me, which made me feel better at first. The girls greeted me warmly and made me feel comfortable as I continued to take everything in.

After the group had chatted for a while, Prudy stood up and prepared to leave. She leaned in, said goodbye, and mentioned that she would come back to check how things were going. It felt like déja vu hearing her say those words to me again. She walked out the door and I was left to begin a new chapter.

I sat quietly for a moment, and then Sarah asked me to follow her. She led me down a long hallway to show me the bedroom that she and I would share. Norma followed us into the room and brought my belongings. They showed me where I could place my things. I didn't have much, just some clothes and, of course, my pink cat. None of the toys that I'd had before were brought with us for this move.

When we had finished unpacking, we went to the kitchen to help Norma prepare dinner. We were having tacos that night, and everyone pitched in to get things ready. It was kind of fun because it helped me to keep my mind off things for the moment. I had the task of helping Sarah set the table, and she made sure to point out where everyone would sit, including me. While we ate dinner, everyone chatted among themselves and then turned their attention to me. They asked me what kind of interests I had and what I liked to do for fun. The first thing that popped into my head was that I loved soccer and riding bikes. That connected with the other girls, and we made a plan to head outside after dinner. I thought that would happen soon, since everyone was done eating their dinner.

As it turned out, we weren't quite done with the meal. I was quickly introduced to a family ritual that occurred nightly without fail. Ruth or Janet would make hot tea, and the family would stay at the table to drink tea and eat a dessert. I had never had hot tea in my life, so that was a first!

When we were done with the tea, everyone helped to clean up and then Sarah and I went outside and rode our bikes until the sun went down.

After heading back into the house, we found that everyone had gathered to watch TV. Before doing that, I asked Norma if I could make a phone call and she nodded yes. I found a phone in the next room and called my friend Kristen. We talked for a while and caught up, which made me feel good. I told her about the new family, and as I continued, I started to break down and cry. My emotions had built up and suddenly were being released as I told her what had happened. I didn't realize it, but Norma had walked into the room and quickly headed over to me. She then told me that I needed to hang up the phone. I told Kristen I had to go and gently put the phone down.

I realized then that I felt drained from everything that had occurred that day. I told Norma I was going to get ready for bed, and she nodded with approval. After I crawled into bed, it felt like I had a million thoughts spinning around in my head. I was in a house full of people that I had just met that day, and I was starting over again. Why did this continue to happen to me? Was the constant moving ever going to stop? I closed my eyes and tried to calm my thoughts. Finally I rolled over and clutched my pink stuffed cat as I cried myself to sleep.

𝓟
THE EXAMPLES
AROUND YOU

As I continued through grade school, my neighborhood friends and their parents played a big role in shaping my outlook. Let's be clear: we moved forward and lived our lives. I was still a kid and had no say in things. And I still wanted to have fun, just like any other kid would. That meant hanging out with my friends, which at times meant spending time with their parents, too. I would spend afternoons or weekends playing with my friends at my house or theirs. Parents coordinated many of our activities so they would know where we were and what we were doing.

We were reaching fifth and sixth grades, and those years with my friends were a lot of fun. They were filled with trips to the comic book store, sleeping over at each other's houses, and watching countless movies. All of this was, of course, intertwined with endless hours of conversation.

Greg, W.C., and Gerilyn were my neighborhood friends, and they are still close to me to this day. The adventures we had on our street were endless. Whether we were riding our bikes continuously up and down our street, playing countless games of baseball or kickball, or just sitting on the porch and talking, we had fun. Those moments filled our childhoods with plenty of great memories. My friends and their parents started to inform my outlook on how different families treated each other. Watching them was like looking through a window into how parents and their children could interact. I would compare their interactions with my own home life.

Our family's dynamics had shifted. The relationship between my parents and I had changed. Were we carrying on like normal? Yes, by all accounts. Subconsciously, though, things had changed. My defenses were up. A wall of protection had grown strong inside of me. Even as those defenses had risen, I still longed for a normal family life. Now I could see glimpses of what that looked like by watching my friends and their parents. Coincidentally, my three friends' families were Catholic. They had shifted from the public grade school that we all attended to a Catholic school not far from where we lived. We didn't see each other in school anymore, but we could be together in our neighborhood. I watched as their families attended weekly Mass together. They were growing up in the church and now had a school to attend that could continue to support their beliefs. I thought that was cool. Their families were tight, and this wrapped things together even more for them. By contrast, my family had stopped attending church after Melyssa left. We had grown up attending our Baptist church weekly, and now we had completely broken free from any connection to it.

This was one of the first times I started to think about the role faith played in my life. It planted a seed that would grow and be addressed a few short years later. At that point in my life, though, I didn't mind not going to church since it meant I didn't have to get up early on Sundays! On the other hand, I was watching my close friends attend church as well as a

Catholic school, and their families seemed closer than ever. This started to register with me. I envied the bonds that they had formed. I envied the shared experiences that they were going through together. It felt good to be around them and to interact with their families. Thankfully my friends' parents have always been welcoming and treated me like a member of their family. Their influence on me was great, and I would draw from it as I moved forward.

M

MODEL CITIZEN

Prudy stopped by the house to check on me maybe twice more. She would ask me how things were going with the family. I told her about my daily routines, which included walking to the pool and playing with the other girls. I didn't have anything negative to say, so I would tell her things were great and that I liked where I was. After those two visits, I didn't see Prudy again. I took that as a sign that I was here to stay.

Summer vacation allowed me to spend time with the family and to continue to acclimate to my new surroundings. I didn't feel much pressure, as we could take the days slowly and we didn't have to be anywhere in particular. Before long, summer started to wind down, and I started to anticipate the beginning of a new school year.

I was heading into the fourth grade at Wake Robin Elementary School, which was located just down the hill from our house. It was close enough that Sarah and I could walk to school, which made it fun for us each day. Janet went to Logan Fontenelle Middle School, which was also close and allowed her to walk as well. Ruth went to Bellevue East High School and could drive herself to and from school. We all had our own paths to school and had built our own daily routines.

Sarah and I were in the same grade but in different classes, which was nice because it gave us some space. I liked that separation because it made me feel like I had my own experiences to share each day.

A fun school memory was being able to walk home for lunch. Our goal was to make it back to school in time to play on the playground before the bell rang to begin the second half of the day. Norma always had our lunch ready as soon as we walked in the door, so we didn't waste time!

I loved going to school and started to make friends with several classmates. It felt like I was settling in, and I could allow myself to relax just a bit. I liked where I was living and going to school, and I was starting to feel normal.

Not long after I started fourth grade, something happened that made me really feel like things were going to work out. Norma and Gary told me they were going to make me a citizen of the United States. I didn't understand what they meant, as I thought I already was a citizen! As we discussed it, one of the things that got my attention was that they said they were also changing the spelling of my name. They were going to take the "y" out and replace it with an "i." I was going from "Melyssa" to "Melissa." I didn't think too much about it, so I just said, "Okay." I immediately asked if I could also change my middle name to "Ann" because I didn't like "Dawn" anymore. It reminded me of Don Unrau, from the previous family I was with, and I didn't want anything to do with them. They said, "Yes, of course," and it was added to the to-do list.

As we continued the conversation, Norma proceeded to say, "You should have become a citizen long ago. Apparently, the Butlers didn't think it was important enough for you to become a citizen, or even care about you, so we are doing this for you." That really hit me in a way that I didn't expect. Her words were meant to cast doubt about my life with the Butlers, as if I never had meant much to them. I didn't believe that. I knew how much my brother loved me, as I did him. If anything, the conversation was confusing for a moment as I didn't understand how the process of becoming a U.S. citizen even worked, but I was still excited to move forward.

It felt like such a special day when we were finally able to go to the courthouse. I thought I was going with the sole purpose of becoming a citizen. It was true that I was gaining citizenship, but I was also joining a family. I was officially being adopted by the Fliehmanns. I was on cloud nine! I kept saying, "Wow!" as I thought about the fact that this family really liked me and wanted me as one of their own!

As I took all of this in, I kept thinking that it was such a relief since it was now official. The relief came because I knew that it meant I wouldn't get packed up and moved on to another family. Things were finally falling into place.

After the citizenship ceremony, I went to school to find that my class had made me a card. They also held a small party for me! It was a special day for sure.

M

A SHIFT

I t was very common for us to go on a lot of outings as a family. Whether it was a normal errand or doing something fun, we ended up doing it together. Every Saturday we would head to the local mall to go shopping and browse the stores that we liked. My new parents would give us some money and let us decide how to spend it. It wasn't a lot, but it was enough to pick up some sweet treats at the candy store! Quite often, the other three girls would go shopping, and I would head off with Gary to sit in a bar, drink Shirley Temples, and watch football. I loved spending one-on-one time with him, as it made me feel like I was the center of attention. I was beginning to feel more connected within the family, and small moments like this made a difference.

The holidays were a fun time as well, especially as all of us girls worked together to bake cookies and decorate. Christmas was spent together at home, and we never had to travel or have any extended family visit, either. Gary was from Michigan and didn't have a strong connection with any remaining family. Since Norma was originally from England, it was difficult for her to travel there or for her family to visit us. To make up for that, Norma's mother would visit in the summer and stay for about three weeks, which was fun as I got to know her.

Another way that I started to feel like I was growing closer to the family was through helping Norma style her hair. She would get her hair set every Friday morning at the salon. This would give her the style she wanted to wear for the week, and after getting it "set" she didn't have to do much to it. A few times mid-week she would ask me to touch her hair up with the curling iron. I was a quick study and got the hang of it after a few attempts. It was my first opportunity to style someone else's hair, and I think that is where I learned to love doing hair. In a way, it became a bonding time for the two of us. By touching up her hair, I made her feel pretty, and in those moments I knew I made her happy.

As time went on, I felt like I had blended into the family and things felt good. We had shared many fun experiences together, and my relationship with each family member was growing stronger.

The good times stood out, and those memories stayed strong. As good as those times were, there were noticeable moments that weren't so good.

Things started to change when I was in fifth grade. Ruth, who was in high school at the time, had become very independent. As a result of that, she and Norma would disagree about virtually everything that Ruth did. Those disagreements would escalate into arguments that resulted in them yelling at each other. That would lead to Gary and Norma getting into an argument, because Norma felt that Gary was taking Ruth's side. Often, right after these arguments, Norma would get a migraine headache. Some of her headaches were so bad that she ended up being hospitalized, while others caused her to have seizures in the middle of the night. On a few of those occasions, she had to be taken to the hospital in an ambulance.

On one of my birthdays Norma was in the hospital because of her headaches and couldn't celebrate with us.

When Norma was hospitalized, Ruth took over and cared for us. She stepped up and made sure we got to school, meals were made, and that the household felt as normal as it could be.

The arguments between Ruth and Norma continued to grow in intensity. They would argue over everything, whether it was about the time of day when Ruth would leave the house and return, or what Ruth was wearing, or how she needed to do more cleaning in the house. The conflict ultimately led to one final blowout. The yelling match hit a peak that led to Ruth packing her things and storming out of the house. She ended up moving in with a friend and never coming back. She had finished high school at that point and was working at a bank. After that day, I never saw Ruth again. I wondered if this was how Patrick had felt when I left, never be seen again. It messes with your head when someone who is living in the same household is gone in an instant and never heard from again. It was hard to watch this scene play out and then compare it to what I had already lived through.

After Ruth left, it was quieter than usual around the house. Norma and Gary didn't speak for days, and the rest of us walked around on eggshells. We didn't want Norma to get upset with any of us. No one knew how things were going to play out, and no one wanted to be the one who caused more trouble.

As the days passed, things started to get back to normal, and the mood in the house relaxed a bit. We all moved on, but we carried a loss within us that we didn't speak about.

$\mathcal{P}$
MIDDLE SCHOOL

As I entered middle school, the silent divide between my parents and me remained strong. If anything, it continued to grow. As a teenager, I was forming my own opinions and finding my own voice. I began to look for new ways to cope with my bottled-up emotions. Music became an important outlet for me. By now, I could start to understand the lyrics, and this helped as I found other voices that could express how I was feeling. The lyrics were one thing, and the style of music was another. I listened to virtually everything. My stereo was my own personal jukebox, and it was set to "shuffle" all the time! I would jump from alternative to metal, from punk to pop, with a dose of country scattered in. I was open to listening to anything, and my speakers were pumping as I rolled through all of it!

It was fun, but something else was happening. The music had turned into a coping mechanism. I could listen to a certain band and get some of my anger out and then shift to another band and release any sorrow that I was feeling. Music has continued to be a support system for me throughout my life. I can pinpoint a specific time period in my life, and there is a "soundtrack" that accompanies it that came straight out of my record collection. I dove into the deep end of the music pool and have stayed there since.

I was also hitting a stage where I cared about how I looked and what other people thought of me... specifically, girls. During this period, I met my first real girlfriend. Shout out to Deb for the countless hours on the phone and millions of love notes! This was important as we dated for just over a year. It was my first opportunity to experience a romantic relationship and the feelings that went with it. Not unlike many kids in junior high, I went through emotional ups and downs with these experiences. I made my way through the relationship by trial and error, and I felt like I was riding on an emotional rollercoaster.

This stage of life helped to solidify friendships as well. I was forming bonds with friends at school over music, my neighborhood friendships remained strong, and now I was entering the world of teenage dating. These relationships were a welcome distraction from home life. They filled my time and kept my mind occupied. Schoolwork, music, books, and an array of friends kept me going day and night. All of it provided an escape and opened me up to thinking about the future. It gave me hope when I needed it.

I have been asked how much I thought about Melyssa during these years. This is often followed by a question about how I dealt with my feelings about her as well as my feelings toward my parents and my younger sister. Of course I thought about Melyssa. I wondered where she was and what she was doing. I wondered if she thought about me and our family. I wondered if she wanted things to go back to the way they had been just as much as I did. I missed her terribly. The wound remained raw, since it had never been dealt with properly.

My parents continued with their lives, and nothing was discussed. Watching them act that way made me angry, and in turn, created distance in our relationship. My younger sister Dere was in grade school, and we barely interacted. We were in completely different places at that point in our lives. The age gap accentuated the distance between us, and we never grew close. I kept my guard up, as I still was fearful of being hurt. I wasn't receiving any counseling, and I didn't have an opportunity to speak with anyone who would understand. Even if I did have someone to talk to, I felt ashamed about what had happened in our family. Sharing it with someone else would have been unthinkable. I didn't have anyone to confide in, so I channeled my sorrow and anger into music and books that helped me escape. Music and friends were the bright spots that gave me something to hold on to.

M

READY FOR SCHOOL

We were now drifting toward the end of summer and starting to think about the new school year. A few days before school began, a list would be posted in a window on one of the front doors of the school. The list showed the classroom rosters. We anxiously waited to see who our sixth-grade teacher would be and if our friends would be in our class. We ran down to the school so we could quickly read each list. I was excited because I liked the kids in my class and couldn't wait to see them again.

Even though I was excited to see my friends, I didn't feel like I was in the popular crowd. I was eleven, and at that age those friendship groups were becoming important. The popular kids had been together longer, and I wanted to figure out a way for them to let me in. This was the year it was going to happen! I knew that I wasn't going to be shipped off to another family, and it was finally my chance to make friendships that would last. Sarah and I were in different classrooms again, and she had her own close group of friends. I was hoping to fit into a group that I could call my own as well.

I remember being so eager for the first day of school that I packed all my school supplies in my backpack the day before and carefully chose the new outfit I was going to wear. Sarah and I walked to school early because I didn't know if we would be able to choose our seats and I didn't want to be the last one trying to find somewhere to sit.

As I walked into the classroom, I found the desks had seat assignments in alphabetical order, and I was in the front row. It took away my anxiety about finding a seat, but now I was seated front and center.

The first few weeks went by quickly, and things felt okay, but not great. The schoolwork was fine, and I kept up, but I kept thinking things would be different socially. I had friends, but not close ones. Everyone was nice to me, but it didn't seem like I was part of the popular group. I wasn't getting invited to sleepovers or some of the birthday parties. I started wondering if it was because I looked different from most of the other girls. Was it because I was Asian and adopted? Or was it because my hair or clothes weren't right?

I was always embarrassed because I had to wear the same outfit twice during the week. Norma wouldn't let us wear multiple outfits, so we had to wear the same thing on a different day of the week. We would space them out as far as we could to make it seem like it was fresh. I took it a step further and stuffed a shirt in my backpack on the day when I had to repeat an outfit. As soon as I got to school, I would run to the bathroom and change my shirt so nobody would make fun of me. I was trying to do whatever I could to fit in. I wasn't just fitting into a new family, I was trying to fit into a good group of friends.

M

A BAD SIGN

One of the activities that we took part in was a school choir concert. Most of the grade levels were involved, and we rehearsed for a few months prior to performing in a concert for our families and friends.

The concert was coming up, and I was very excited because I had been chosen to hold up a sign during one of the songs. Norma and Gary were always good about coming to our school events, so I was looking forward to playing an extra part in this program.

I felt nervous excitement as I walked with my class onto the stage. We stood in our positions and waited for the music to begin. As my class sang our song, I waited for the cue to lift my sign.

My time finally arrived, and I proudly held my sign up high. I sang and held my arms up straight as I played my part. There was one small issue with my performance, though. I had accidentally held my sign backwards. The audience saw a blank card instead of the picture on the other side. I had no clue this had happened as I brought the sign back down and continued to sing the song. I was excited as we left the school, and no one mentioned my mistake.

The next morning at breakfast, I found out that my mistake had made Norma very angry. As she began to speak, I had a sinking feeling as I realized I had disappointed her and now everyone was going to hear about it.

Norma described what I had done and went on to tell me how "dumb" I was and how much of a "disappointment" I was to her: "You only had one job and couldn't do it." I tried to hold back my tears because I didn't want to look like I had been crying when I arrived at school, but I tears started rolling down my cheeks. The next thing I knew, Norma slapped my face and told me to stop crying. I was shocked that she had slapped me. She was upset about the mistake I had made, and because I had started to cry, she had become so angry that she had actually hit me. I narrowed my eyes slightly as I looked up at her. I wanted her to know how angry I was, and glaring at her was the only way I could do it.

Norma told Sarah to leave for school so she wouldn't be late. When the room cleared, she turned back to me and continued to yell. I just looked away from her as my anger grew. After a few minutes I got up from the table and told her I was going to school. This infuriated her, so she stepped forward and grabbed me by my ponytail and yanked me back to the chair I had been sitting on. I squirmed to get away, but she pushed me into the chair and told me to sit down because I wasn't going anywhere. I gave up and sat at the table while she continued to tell me what an idiot I was.

When she was finally done, I went to my room and sat on my bed in a daze. I was in shock about what had just happened. How had things reached this point? The night before had been so much fun! I had been so excited to sing in the choir and hold my sign up. I'd had no idea that I made a mistake that would have led to this. I was also terribly hurt by what Norma had said to me. Being called "dumb" and an "idiot" by the person who was supposed to be my mother triggered my worst fears. If she felt that way about me, would she now find a way to get rid of me like the other families had done? I was scared and didn't move as I kept replaying everything that had happened.

Norma called the school and told them I would be in after lunch that day. I spent the morning on my bed until Sarah came home from school for lunch. After lunch we walked back to school together. I tried to pull myself together as we walked in silence toward the school. I didn't want to cry or to let anyone know what had happened to me, so I kept quiet as much as possible.

I wish I could say this incident was the only time I was yelled at, but it wasn't. Norma blew up at us a lot, and Janet and I were usually the targets of her anger. Sarah never experienced what the two of us did, and it started to become apparent that Norma favored her. I started to feel resentment toward Sarah as I watched the favoritism play out.

I don't think Gary was truly aware of what happened at home after he went to work. When he came home from work, Norma acted like nothing had happened. As this pattern continued, resentment made me shut down. I limited some of my interactions with the family and tried not to speak to anyone if I could help it. We all had different things going on in our lives, so it was easy to stay quiet and keep under the radar. I was trying to lay low and avoid confrontations as much as possible. My defenses were up, and I felt like I was constantly looking over my shoulder.

$\mathcal{P}$
HAVING SOME FAITH IN HIGH SCHOOL

igh school is always a hot topic when I get together with my friends. We have a ton of crazy stories to tell from that time period. Obviously, many things were starting to change at this stage of our lives. These were the years where we were trying to figure out who we were. Our bodies were changing, and our minds were exploring new ideas. We were trying to figure out where we were going and what we wanted to do with our lives. Well, in theory we were. In reality, I had no idea where I was going, but I wanted to get out of the house as soon as possible.

My sophomore year proved to be a turning point. I was almost 16, and high school seemed overwhelming. My grades were average. I was just getting by. The reports from my teachers at conferences always seemed to have a similar theme: "Patrick has the capability to do his work at a high level but doesn't put forth the effort." I was an avid reader and could keep up with anything that was asked of me. I knew I was smart enough to do the work. Technically there wasn't a problem, and my teachers and parents knew it. The truth was that

I just didn't care about getting good grades. I had no motivation, and no one was truly guiding me. The only thing my parents could do was sit me down repeatedly and browbeat me with questions like "Why don't you care more about this?" or "Why don't you try harder?" That line of questioning didn't work for them or for me.

When they realized that their questions had no effect, they found a different way to motivate me. During my sophomore year I discovered the drama department and enrolled in Drama and Stagecraft. Drama class focused on acting, while Stagecraft focused on the production elements of a stage play. I loved both of them! They were the only classes I cared about. So my parents gave me an ultimatum: "Get decent grades in all of your classes or we will pull you from Drama and Stagecraft." Surprise, surprise! My grades quickly rose until the pressure from my parents was no longer needed. I was free to focus on something I was passionate about.

Greg Doty was my teacher, and he had a vast amount of experience in the theater world. He became a mentor, and his belief in me was a boost that I needed. Over the course of three years, I worked tirelessly building sets, running lights, and grabbing roles in school plays and musicals. Mr. Doty may not have realized it, but the years I spent learning from him had a positive impact on me at a time when I needed it. He was a father, and between raising his kids and also teaching high schoolers, he had developed a fantastic approach to dealing with younger people. He showed me that a man can teach, share, and interact with kids in a way that is encouraging and empowering. I didn't get that positive reinforcement from my own father, and I was grateful to learn from Mr. Doty.

The theater program was a huge influence on me, but it wasn't the only positive influence. During my sophomore year, my childhood friends invited me to join a weekly youth group they had been attending. Every Wednesday night, they would go to St. Leo Catholic Church to participate in a high school youth group. I knew that they had been going for a while, and it sounded like fun based on the stories they shared with me. I now had a chance to take part in something that was having a great influence on my friends. I was nervous at first, because I was afraid that I wouldn't belong. The kids in the youth group lived within the boundaries of the St. Leo parish and attended different Catholic high schools. To my surprise, I was accepted, and it didn't matter that I attended a public high school.

The weekly gathering quickly became the highlight of the week for me and my friends. We looked forward to seeing our friends from different schools and taking part in the activities that the group leaders had prepared. Each week the activities were slightly different, but certain elements never changed. One of the main purposes of the group was to bring kids together and give them an outlet to connect and be heard. The meetings were held at a Catholic church, so there was an underlying Christian theme, but we weren't beat over the head with it. Besides, the kids who typically attended were already Catholic. They already understood and lived by many of the values and themes that were discussed.

As the weeks passed, it was easy for me to fit in, and I started to feel comfortable. Over time I realized that attending youth group meetings had started to make me consider my own faith as I watched how the other kids were able to express theirs. On any given group night, we would break into small groups and discuss a topic that was relevant to us as teenagers. The discussions gave us an opportunity to share how we felt. The openness of the group was amazing to me. Seeing other kids my age be vulnerable and share their thoughts shocked me at first. We talked about fears and anxieties that we felt as teenagers or peer pressures that we felt at school.

The group leaders played a major role in establishing an environment where kids felt comfortable sharing how they truly felt. They moderated the conversations and offered great insight when we needed it. The Youth Ministry leader was Karen Mackey. She and her husband Bill led the adult leaders and paved the way for their team to stay consistent when guiding us in our discussions. I was quickly drawn to them, and our friendship would grow during the three years that I was involved with the group. The group leaders set an example for all of us that showed how adults could relate on levels that we didn't think possible at the time.

The weekly group meetings felt like a breath of fresh air to me. I could actually talk about things and not feel judged or nervous about how someone might react. Even though I was starting to feel safe, I didn't discuss the situation concerning Melyssa. My worst fear was having my friends hear the story and look at me or my family differently. The friends that I was starting to make in the youth group were amazing people, and I wanted to fit in. The shame I felt about my family was strong, and I didn't want anyone to see it. Nevertheless, we talked about everything else and supported each other. The youth group was scheduled to meet during the school year, which meant we would take a break during the summer and then pick up again in the fall. Summer was approaching, and I could finally drive, which would provide even more opportunities to socialize. Things were starting to open up for me.

M

SNEAKING OUT

When I was in junior high school, I finally started to form friendships that went deeper than my day-to-day interactions with kids at school. One of my close friends, Jennifer, was Filipino and so beautiful that I felt plain in comparison.

Luckily there was more to our friendship than looks. Jennifer was one of the first real friends I had. She and I talked constantly, and I loved being able to finally connect with someone. Sometimes I went to sleepovers at her house, and it was fun to spend time with a completely different family. I thought Jennifer's mom and dad were cool, and I could see that they respected her and allowed her to be who she wanted to be without judgment. This was very different from how I was treated by my family. I was envious and wished that my parents treated me with even a fraction of the respect shown by Jennifer's parents.

Finally I was able to return the favor and invite Jennifer and her cousin Shawn to sleep over at my house after our junior high dance. It was the first time I would have friends over to spend the night, so I was excited!

We came home from the dance and laughed as we replayed everything that had happened that night. That was fun, but it was only part of what we had planned for the evening. Earlier in the week, we had decided that we could have even more fun if we sneaked out to meet some of our other friends at Jennifer's house. The success of our plan depended on the three of us sleeping in the basement of my house and then sneaking out after Norma, Gary, and Sarah had fallen asleep.

Sleeping in the basement would make it easier for us to leave the house and come back without anyone noticing we had been gone. We put on our pajamas and watched a movie to pass the time until we could leave. When we thought everyone had fallen asleep, we quickly started changing into our clothes so we could head out. Just as we were about to leave, Norma walked down the steps into the basement. I couldn't believe she had caught us, and I'm sure I looked like a deer in headlights. She asked what we were doing, and we quickly made up the excuse that we were having a fashion show. Norma ordered us to change into our pajamas and settle down for the night. Her tone struck fear into us, and we knew we had to do as she said. We didn't go anywhere beyond those basement walls that night. We couldn't figure out how Norma had found out about our plans, but then it occurred to us that Sarah must have said something to her. I had trouble falling asleep that night because I knew what the next day was going to bring.

The next morning, right after Jennifer and Shawn had left, Norma started in on me. When Gary heard the commotion, he walked into the room and wanted to know what we were doing. Norma told him about walking in on us the night before. I told him we had been having a "fashion show" and he believed me, but Norma knew I wasn't telling the truth. Sarah had told her the real story, and she was not going to let it go.

Gary had been getting ready to leave the house that morning. He said he needed to run some errands, but I'm sure he wanted to avoid getting into an argument with Norma.

As soon as Gary had left, Norma started yelling at me. She got so close to my face that we were practically touching. She was close enough that I could smell the coffee on her breath, and I stepped backward to get away from her. When I moved away, she punched me and then grabbed my hair. She pulled me back in close so she could continue to yell in my face. At that moment, I deeply resented Sarah for telling on me. At the same time, I felt anger building up inside me. I wanted to punch Norma and defend myself, but I was scared to do it.

When Norma had finally finished yelling at me, I went to my bedroom. It was a sunny day, and I knew that Norma would eventually head outside to work in her flower garden. After she left the house, I went into Norma and Gary's bedroom and opened the bottom drawer of her dresser where she kept the baby book that Prudy had sent with me when I arrived at their home. Inside the book were all of my baby pictures as well as pictures of my first family, the Butlers. There was also a book that Jack and Jan Hinze had made for me of their family when I had stayed with them in Iowa.

As I sat and looked at the pictures, my heart felt sad and I wanted to be back with any of them right then. Oh, how I missed Patrick. I wished I could see him. I wanted to return to a time when things had felt normal and safe. I didn't look at the books for too long because I wasn't supposed to know they were there. I looked long enough to hold onto some good memories and then put the books in the drawer and headed back to my room. While I had been looking at the pictures, I had thought about trying to find Prudy, but I didn't think I would be able to contact her because she had stopped checking in on me after I was adopted. I felt so alone.

I remember going back to school on Monday and talking with Jennifer and Shawn in the hallway. They asked if I had gotten into trouble. I told them that Norma had yelled at me for a bit, but then it was over. They said Norma had looked scary and that they had been sure I was going to be in a lot of trouble.

That botched sleepover was the last time Jennifer and Shawn ever came over to my house. We remained friends, but Norma told me I was forbidden to spend the night at Jennifer's house. If Norma could have ended my friendship with Jennifer and Shawn she would have done it, but I wouldn't let that happen. Norma tried to forbid me to be friends with quite a few people, but I never listened to her. She could control what happened inside the house, but she couldn't control every part of my life, especially my friendships.

WHEELS, ODD JOBS, AND INDEPENDENCE

Having my own car felt like winning the lottery! It meant I could get out of the house, pick up my friends, and we could cruise wherever we wanted. My newfound freedom felt amazing, and I wanted to drive everywhere! Eventually I realized I would need money to continue doing this, and that was when my job hunt started. Throughout high school I found part-time jobs wherever I could. I bagged groceries, worked in a dry cleaner with my childhood friends W.C and Gerilyn (sharing more laughs than I can tell you about!), and worked in a bowling alley. Basically, I worked wherever I could. My goal was to earn enough money to buy gas, pay for car insurance, and still have a little left over for music or comic books.

Having a car brought independence, and that meant everything to me. Instead of being confined to my house, I could be out having fun. Need a ride? No problem! Let me swing over and pick you up! Summer was a blast as I learned how to navigate the roads with my friends.

When summer ended and I entered my junior year of high school, I felt increasingly distant from my parents. We didn't talk much, and our conversations never went beneath the surface. The same held true with my younger sister, Dere, as the gap between our ages gave us nothing to discuss.

I didn't feel close to anyone in my family, so I spent most of my time away from them. To avoid tension at home, I would jump in my car and drive wherever I wanted to go. I could crank up the radio and clear my head as I cruised the streets. If I had to spend time at home, I was usually in my room listening to music or reading. Either way, my goal was to escape into my own world and avoid facing my negative feelings toward my parents. Most of those feelings involved anger or shame.

My mind was still filled with questions about Melyssa. She was out there somewhere, and it felt like she was a world away. At this point I was 16 going on 17, and Melyssa was in her mid-teens as well. What was she doing? Was she okay? Was she happy? Did she miss me? Did she miss our family? I felt like I would never know the answers to those questions, so I might as well keep my thoughts to myself. Burying my thoughts and feelings took some effort. Keeping busy helped, so I tried to do just that.

As time passed, I started to notice details about my parents. Specifically, I watched how they interacted with each other and I concluded that they weren't happy with their relationship or with themselves.

As is true in many families, money was a frequent source of conflict. Both of my parents worked full time, and my dad also picked up a part-time job bartending a few nights a week to supplement their income. One of my fun memories was helping him count the coins that he brought home in his tip jar. He made it clear that every dollar was important. Watching him work two jobs left a lasting impression on me. My father showed me the importance of working hard to provide for his family. Those lessons have stayed with me to this day, and I give him credit for his influence.

I was not close to my dad, but he still had an influence on me. He worked hard in both of his jobs, and my mother was successful in her full-time job with the school system. Earning enough money wasn't easy, but they were able to keep us afloat.

I could sense ongoing tension between my parents, and I knew that it wasn't just about money. Sometimes my mother would make a sarcastic remark to my father and he would respond with a similar verbal jab. They may have believed that their comments passed over my head, but I easily picked them up. I knew that they weren't happy in their marriage and that they were not addressing their feelings toward each other.

Watching my parents interact with each other left a lasting impression on me. It is something that I think of often as an adult. I remember how their relationship slowly fell apart over time. I recall their fights and bitter comments. I witnessed how they walked past each other many times without saying a word. Not only could I sense the tension between them, but I could also see the utter sadness that showed up in so many ways. They would try to put on a positive face, but they were unable to hide the depression that existed beneath the surface. My father did his best to focus on what was in front of him, but my mother struggled with anxiety and would continue to battle depression for the rest of her life.

P
RESTORING SOME FAITH

O ver the course of my high school years, I continued to attend youth group meetings with my friends. In doing so, I thought about my faith and what it meant to me. After Melyssa had been removed from our lives, our family had stopped attending weekly church services at the Baptist church we had attended since I was a child. As I went through middle school and the beginning of high school, religion did not play a key role in my life. I wasn't attending church, and my family did not have any discussions about religion or faith. As I continued to struggle with the feelings that I had bottled up, I started to wonder about the influence of religion, church, and faith in my life. I continued to think about these topics and then I talked with Karen and Bill Mackey, the leaders of our youth group. They encouraged me to do some investigating on my own and to ask as many questions as I could think of along the way.

My search began with visits to several churches. I met with pastors and priests and asked them about their denominations. I saved the Catholic church for last. I had been attending the youth group at St. Leo, which is a Catholic church, for two years, but I wanted to make an unbiased decision about my faith. One of the best pieces of advice that I received came from a Catholic priest, however. When I went to him and said, "There are so many churches and religions in the world; which one should I choose?" he replied, "You should choose the one that will allow you to best express your faith." The more I thought about what he had said, the more it made sense to me.

Not long after doing some of my research on different faith traditions, I walked into our Wednesday night youth group meeting and went straight to Karen and announced, "I know what I want to do!" She excitedly asked what my decision was, and I quickly said, "I want to be part of the Catholic church." I also asked her if she would help me along the way. She said, "Yes, of course." After learning about the classes that would lead to my confirmation, I asked Karen if she would be my sponsor. She said yes again, and my journey began.

I was set to attend RCIA (Rite of Christian Initiation of Adults) classes, followed by a confirmation Mass that would take place at Easter. I began attending classes with Karen but had not mentioned much to my family. As the date of my confirmation approached, I told my parents what I was doing and mentioned that I hoped they would attend the Mass to observe my confirmation. My dad told me that if I wanted to join the Catholic faith, he would support my decision. My mother, however, was adamantly against it and said she would not attend my confirmation. I was shocked and confused by her disapproval. Our family had not attended a church together in eight years. The topic of religion was not discussed regularly in our house. I was pursuing my faith in a Christian church, and suddenly that was a bad thing? What was happening?

My mother's refusal to support my decision made me angry, and I became even more determined to forge ahead. The gap between my mother and me had been wide, and now it had blown open even more. I had carried the hurt from Melyssa's disconnection for years. I was joining a faith tradition to heal my pain, while my mother had turned her back on religion. Her reaction troubled me, and I felt more disconnected from her than ever before. I would be turning 18 soon, and I was making up my mind about which direction I wanted to go. It became clear to me that I wanted to move away from home.

I was fortunate to have many friends and family members who did support my decision. My father attended the Mass along with all of my friends. The guidance of Karen and Bill Mackey during my journey is something that I will never forget. Their friendship was crucial. They provided a strong example of a marriage steeped in faith and mutual support. It was a positive influence when I needed it most. I was now a Catholic, I was 18, and I was moving on.

M

RUN

I was looking forward to entering high school because it meant I would be able to do the things I was interested in while gaining some freedom from the control I felt at home.

I began my high school journey at Bellevue East. One of the reasons I was excited to attend East was the strength of their marching band. I had played the flute and piccolo since the sixth grade, and I hoped my skills would be good enough to let me join the band. Tryouts came and went, and I was able to join the band. I was thrilled! Being in band would help me make friends while doing something I loved.

Band practices took up a lot of time, but I didn't mind because the practices gave me a chance to be with friends and to feel like I had some freedom. Our main focus was getting ready for the halftime shows for our football games as well as band competitions. I loved being part of something so big and knowing that I had played a role in our success. Our band did well and ended up winning several competitions. The first year that I marched, we performed music from the Phantom of the Opera. It was amazing to see the music come to life through our huge band and the structured movements we made across the entire playing field.

Being part of the band was a major commitment. We couldn't miss practice, and we definitely couldn't miss a game or a competition. I came close to missing a competition one time, though, and it was a reminder that my world was split into two very different realities. My school and band life were my calm outlet, while my home life could turn controlling and chaotic in an instant.

We were out of school on winter break, and it was the day before the band would be involved in a big competition. I was excited because we had been performing well and I felt like we had a good chance to win. It was a Friday morning, and Sarah and I were getting our cereal and making coffee and toast for Norma before she woke up.

As Norma made her way into the kitchen, she immediately started lecturing Sarah and me about something she thought we had done. I must have raised my eyebrows in response to something she said, and that was all it took to infuriate her. Suddenly she slapped my face and said, "Don't you look at me that way, you idiot." I couldn't believe this was happening at 9:00 in the morning! I sat in silence as she continued to rant at us. She stood at the edge of the table and yelled about how unappreciative we were and how awful Ruth and Janet had been after she adopted them and made them a home, only to see them move out as soon as they turned 18.

She then turned to me and said, "You can't manage to stop talking in class with your friends. If you weren't talking so much, you would be getting better grades!" At that point I got up from the table and started to leave the room. As I turned to walk away, I felt something hit me in the back of my head, followed by a hit on my back. I bent over and continued to move forward as the blows kept coming. Norma was in a rage as she punched me. I started crying, and I yelled at her to stop hitting me. I dodged her next punch and was able to run out of the kitchen and down the hall to my bedroom. I slammed the door and got dressed as fast as I could. To my relief, Norma didn't follow me into my room. After I was dressed, I ran to the front door, left the house, and ran away as fast as I could.

I didn't know where to go, so I ran down to the elementary school playground. I had no friends to call and didn't know what to do next. I leaned back against a piece of playground equipment and started to cry. I kept asking myself, "Why me?" and finally yelled out, "Why is my life like this? I hate it!" I hated the Butlers for getting rid of me and putting me in this position in the first place. I hated how I had been passed around from family to family. I hated having to live in an abusive household.

I spent a few hours at the playground as I tried to calm myself down. It was Friday, and I knew Norma would spend part of the day getting her hair set at the salon. She would most likely take Sarah with her, and they would end up going to lunch and then shopping. That would give me an opportunity to head home and be left alone.

When I felt the timing was right, I walked home. I knew that the basement door was always unlocked, and I quietly opened it and went inside. I listened for any movement but heard nothing. I had guessed correctly that they would be gone. I went upstairs into the kitchen and grabbed a few things to make a sandwich. I took the food and headed back into the basement. We had a bar with stools that extended along one wall. I put the food behind the bar so I could eat it later. I watched TV all day and thought about what might happen when Norma came home.

Around 4:00 p.m. I heard the garage door open. I quickly turned off the TV and ran behind the bar. My heart was pounding as Norma and Sarah came into the house from the garage and then went upstairs. I wasn't sure what to do next. They knew I had been gone all day and hadn't looked for me. With that thought in my head, I decided to just stay behind the bar.

I kept expecting that someone would come downstairs or that I would hear them talking about where I was. But no one came down the stairs, and things were quiet upstairs. I eventually fell asleep on the floor behind the bar. I woke up a while later and noticed it was dark outside. It was almost 7:00 p.m., and I heard someone let Pepper, our cocker spaniel, outside. I sat up and ate my sandwich in the dark behind the bar. I decided not to go upstairs. Instead, I sat and thought about everything that had happened that day. One thing hit me: they had no idea where I was and apparently didn't really care, because they were carrying on as if everything was okay.

As I sat alone in the dark, I thought about what Patrick might be doing right then and how much I needed to talk to him. I wanted to call the Butlers. I knew their phone number by heart, but I was scared they would tell me never to call them again and hang up on me, so I didn't do it. I also thought about getting in touch with Prudy, and I wished that I knew Jack and Jan Hinze's phone number in Iowa because I was sure they would help me if I needed them. I thought about all of the people who had helped me at various times in my life. I wished desperately that I could be with any of them at that moment.

How had I ended up in the same house with such a controlling, abusive woman?

Suddenly the door to the basement opened. The light came on, and I could hear Norma whistling as she walked down the steps. I knew she was coming down to lock the basement door for the night. I held my breath and didn't move a muscle. Sure enough, she made her way to the outside door and checked the lock. When she saw it was locked, she turned around and went back upstairs. The light clicked off, and then she shut the door. I exhaled slowly and leaned back. I stayed behind the bar and cried myself to sleep that night.

When morning came, I was awakened by footsteps upstairs. I remembered that it was the day of the marching band competition and that I needed to show up on time. I used the bathroom downstairs and then decided to go upstairs and get my flute and walk to the high school.

Norma was surprised to see me, but I walked right past her and into my bedroom where I picked up my flute. I ran to the bathroom and locked the door, then brushed my teeth and combed my hair. It didn't take long before Norma was standing outside the bathroom door and yelling at me to unlock it. I just stood in the bathroom hugging my flute as I tried to figure out how to avoid Norma and get out of the house.

I heard Gary say, "Missy, open up the door," so I reluctantly did. I told him that I was going to the band competition and needed to leave soon. He said, "Go on," and I moved quickly around both of them. I heard Norma screaming at me as I ran out of the house crying. As I was walking down the sidewalk, Gary's car pulled up beside me. He told me to get in so he could drive me to the high school.

After I got into the car, Gary told me that I would need to come home immediately after the competition had ended. He said that Sarah would wait for me and give me a ride home. I nodded in agreement as I opened the car door when we arrived at school. I had no choice. I was at school, and I wanted to go to the competition.

The family knew where I was, and I knew I would have to face them again. At that point, though, all I could think about was Sarah. I resented her so much. I was jealous of her because it seemed that she could do nothing wrong in the eyes of Norma and Gary. She was their favorite and was never touched by the anger that was directed at me. I hated seeing Sarah as the band gathered to board the two buses that would take us to the competition. I prayed that Sarah and I wouldn't be on the same bus. We weren't, and I felt a bit of relief as the buses left the school. It felt good to be out of the house and away from the trouble that surrounded me. I felt like I could breathe for a moment. I could be with friends and focus on something that I enjoyed. This part of the day was mine, and I wanted to hold onto it.

M
CHECK-IN TIME

The day seemed to fly by. The band competition had gone well, and everyone started to pack up their instruments. I suddenly felt a huge surge of anxiety wash over me as I thought about going home. It was a Saturday, so everyone would be home together. Thankfully Gary would be there, and he could protect me from Norma's wrath. I planned to stay close to him and help him with any projects he had on his list for the day. Even if he was just planning to watch a football game, I would stay close to him. I wanted to stay as far away from Norma as possible.

The car ride was quiet as Sarah drove us home. We didn't say a word to each other. I walked into the house and quickly put my things in my bedroom. Thankfully they had fed us at school, so I didn't have to eat at home. I changed into my PJ's and went to bed. I was mentally drained, and my head was pounding.

When I woke up the next morning, I stared at the ceiling and thought about everything that had happened. It wasn't long before I heard Gary making Sunday breakfast for everyone. As I walked into the kitchen, he smiled at me and asked me to chop some onions for a Spanish omelet that he was making.

Everyone gathered at the table for breakfast. As we ate, I stayed silent and made no effort to make eye contact with Norma. I ate quickly and then went back to my bedroom. I spent all day in my room thinking about what had happened. Dinner was a repeat of breakfast, and I continued to stay silent. After dinner, I went to bed. I felt relieved that Gary had been home. He had been the buffer I needed throughout the day.

The next day was Monday. Going to school would allow me to get away again. I was worried about Monday morning, but to my relief Norma stayed in bed. Sarah and I drove to school in silence and went our separate ways quickly. The day seemed to fly by, but I think it felt that way because I dreaded going home. As we pulled up to the house, I noticed that Gary was home earlier than usual. I was happy, though, because I knew Gary could buffer me from Norma.

When I walked into the house, Gary told me to get a snack. He said that we were going somewhere and that we needed to get into the car. Norma, Gary, and I got into the car and we pulled away from the house. I thought Gary wanted me to come with them so they would know where I was. I assumed that when I had "run away," it had caused a conflict between them, and having me ride with them would keep things calm.

We drove for about 30 minutes and then parked in front of a building that looked like a hospital. As we walked through the entrance, I was approached by a woman who looked like a nurse. She asked me what my name was. I was confused about what was going on, but I quietly told her my first and last name. As soon as I said my last name, it set off a chain reaction of activity. I was suddenly whisked away from my parents and taken through a set of doors into another room. I had no clue what was happening. I was in disbelief as I was separated from my parents and now facing two people who I assumed were nurses. I barely had time to think and suddenly felt scared.

I didn't know it at the time, but I quickly found out that the "hospital" that I was in was called Richard Young. It wasn't a hospital in the traditional sense. It was a psychiatric facility for young people.

What would happen to me now?

M

FIRST DAY

After the nurses had taken down my information, we walked down a hallway and entered an office. I was surprised to see my parents and a woman with short, red hair who had a serious, "no-nonsense" look on her face. She stood up, motioned for me to sit down, and introduced herself as Dr. Taylor.

The office was professional looking, yet comfortable. There was a brown leather couch, three leather chairs, a few bookcases, and a small table. From my perspective, the room felt dark and didn't have a happy vibe. I sat down on the leather couch as far away from my parents as possible.

Gary looked as if he had been dragged there against his will. It was clear that his nerves were shot. From my point of view, he had no backbone. What was it with the dads in my life? Not one of them had ever stood up for me when I needed them. They were bullied by their wives and had done whatever they were told to do.

Norma seemed to be playing the part of a caring mother who wanted help for her delinquent teenage daughter. What a crock of shit. She was the one with the mood swings and abusive tendencies, not me.

Dr. Taylor was a psychiatrist, and I had been assigned to her care. She told me she was going to help me get through whatever was going on. Dr. Taylor explained that Richard Young was designed to help teens and young adults with a variety of issues ranging from behavioral problems to substance abuse to mental disorders. It seemed I would be classified as having a behavioral issue.

Dr. Taylor asked Norma and Gary what had happened at home to trigger me into running away. Norma said that we had argued and then I had run out of the house and stayed away for a day. She said I never came home, and she described how worried she and Gary had been about my whereabouts. She looked at me and said that she only wanted the best for me and hoped that I could get the help I needed.

I felt my blood pressure rise as she spoke. As I stared at her, my eyes spoke for me. I hoped that by glaring at her I could let her know how much I hated and resented her at that moment. Dr. Taylor immediately felt the tension in the room, and she asked me if I had anything to say. I looked at her and shook my head no. What was the point? I felt like no matter what I said at that moment, it wouldn't have changed anything. The adults were going to be believed over a child.

I looked at Gary and Norma in disbelief. They had painted a picture of me as a troublesome teenager who had caused all of the issues that had brought us to this hospital. Their description of what had happened suggested that everything was my fault and that they had done nothing to contribute to the problems. They conveniently left out Norma's verbal and physical attacks on me.

We were in the office for about an hour. As Gary and Norma were talking with Dr. Taylor, all I could think about was how things were going to be when we got home that night. I decided that I would ignore them as much as possible. If

I could just keep a low profile, maybe we could find a way to avoid fighting.

Dr. Taylor picked up her phone and said, "We're ready; just come in." I thought, "Oh, no, someone else that we have to talk to." The door opened, and two people in hospital scrubs stood in the doorway. I stared at them and then heard Dr. Taylor say, "Melyssa, you are going with them." I looked at them again and then turned toward Gary and Norma. Gary just stared at the floor, and Norma had a smug look on her face. I knew I didn't have a choice, so I stood up and followed the aides down a hallway and into a small room where I was handed a pair of pants and a hospital gown and was told to put them on. I asked them why I had to change clothes, and they said I was being admitted to the hospital.

As I held the clothes, I suddenly broke into tears. I shut the door, slowly got undressed, and put my other clothes in a bag that they had provided for me. As I put on the gown and pants, my mind raced. Why was I being admitted to a psychiatric hospital? I wasn't the problem, my parents were! I was not crazy, so why was this happening to me? I slowly opened the door and handed the bag of clothing to one of the nurses. I was then taken into a different room where my vitals were taken and I was given a hospital identity wristband. I looked at the wristband and saw that it had my full name, age, and date of birth. I looked up at the nurse and she said, "Everything is going to be okay." I just cried and shook my head in disbelief.

The two nurses then walked me to two large doors and used their badges to open them. The doors opened and we entered a large room. Immediately to our left was a woman seated at a desk behind plexiglass. As she greeted us, I looked around the open space and noticed large couches and chairs of different colors. It looked like a large lounge or family room.

The woman at the desk was named Kate, and in a very calm voice she told me that she was going to take me to my room.

As we walked down the hallway, Kate told me about my room and informed me that I would have a roommate. As she spoke to me, it felt like everything was going in one ear and out the other. I still couldn't believe I was in this building and that this was happening to me.

As we entered my room, I wondered what I would have to get used to now. The room had two beds and an attached bathroom. As Kate was showing me the room, a girl walked in and introduced herself as Nadia. I had just met my new roommate. The day felt like a weird dream that just kept going. Heck, my whole life had started to feel like that.

M

FIRST NIGHT

After I had met Nadia, Kate headed for the door but stopped to tell me that it was time to go eat and that Nadia would help me figure things out. I wasn't very hungry, but I had to go. Nadia and I walked down the hallway and joined seven other kids standing in line. The staff took roll and then swiped their cards to open the doors to the cafeteria.

As we pushed our trays along the counter, we were able to select what we wanted to eat. After choosing my meal, I sat at a table with Nadia and a few others. Someone asked what my name was, and after I told them, everyone at the table took turns introducing themselves. They started asking me questions about who I was and where I came from. I started to feel a bit overwhelmed. I knew that they were just being friendly and I didn't feel pressured, but I felt unsure of everything so I kept quiet. I just wanted to go to my room and sleep.

As I looked at everyone else in the room, I noticed that they were wearing normal clothing. They were dressed like any other teenager would be. It felt like I stuck out since I was wearing a hospital gown and scrub pants. I didn't understand why I had to wear hospital clothes, so I asked Nadia. She said that anyone who was new had to wear them because it would

prevent us from running away and because we were on a suicide alert. I told her I wasn't suicidal, and Nadia said that after
two days I would be allowed to wear normal clothes again. It
hit me that I didn't have any clothes from home. I certainly had
not realized that I needed to pack for this trip! Nadia told me
that my parents would be dropping clothes off if they hadn't
already done so.

After dinner, everyone gathered in the big room. Three
staff members named Kate, Dave, and Terry were in charge
of whatever we were about to do. It turned out that group
meetings were a daily occurrence. We were split into smaller
groups with the purpose of reflecting on our day. The goal was
to talk about what had made us happy, sad, angry, and so on.
My group included two other people who seemed to be about
my age.

The staff member leading our group was Kate. She introduced me to the rest of the group and said I didn't have to talk
in this session. I could listen and watch how the small group
worked. One of the people in my group was a guy named
Steve. At first glance, he reminded me of a "hippie," as he had
medium-length brown hair, large wire-rimmed glasses, and
scruffy facial hair. After telling us about his day, he explained
that he was in this place because he was schizophrenic and was
trying to get back on the medication that would control his
behavior. He had been at Richard Young for two weeks so far.
The other person in our group was a girl named Megan who
had medium-length strawberry blond hair and looked very
normal. She was in for depression and at one point had been
suicidal. She had been there for over three weeks.

As I listened to Steve and Megan, I kept thinking that
they looked like normal people. I was trying to see if anything
stood out that would show me why they were there. Their
outward appearance did not suggest that they were going

through anything. I realized that it's impossible to understand what anyone else is going through based on assumptions and appearance.

I was surprised when Steve and Megan asked me why I was there. I hadn't expected to talk. I didn't know what to say, so I stayed quiet. I had no intention of sharing my experiences or getting close to any of these people.

When the small-group discussion was over, we were able to mingle and talk with each other. I asked Kate if I could go to my room to sleep, and she said we weren't allowed to go to our rooms yet. I looked around and found a place where I could sit and watch everyone else as they talked. Nadia came over and tried to talk with me, but I told her I just wanted to be alone. She said she understood and told me that if I wanted to join them in a game of UNO to come over, but I just shook my head no.

Soon Terry came over and introduced himself to me. He told me how long he had been on the staff at Richard Young and then asked me a few questions about myself. I didn't have much to say and responded with one-word answers like "Yes," "No," and "Maybe." I was hoping that he would get tired of my short answers and walk away, but he continued to ask questions. I soon got annoyed and announced that I was going to sit and watch the UNO game.

At around 9 p.m., we were finally allowed to go to our rooms. I felt relieved and immediately walked back to my room because I wanted to get into bed. When I arrived, I saw a small toiletry bag sitting on my bed. Inside the bag I found a toothbrush, toothpaste, shampoo, conditioner, deodorant, and a bar of soap. Besides my hospital scrubs, that was all I had.

Nadia went into the bathroom and showered first, and when she was finished, I did the same. Then I got into bed and closed my eyes in hopes of making everything go away.

As Nadia turned off the light, she said, "Things will be better tomorrow."

Would they get better? I didn't know what would happen next, but it was clear that this day had gone terribly wrong. I pulled the blanket up to my neck and quietly cried myself to sleep.

M

A NEW WORLD

Morning came quickly, and I didn't feel like I had enough energy to get out of bed. We were awoken by a loud, cheerful voice that took me by surprise. I opened my eyes to see an African American woman wearing bright lipstick and bright-colored glasses. Her voice stood out, and so did her personality. I couldn't help but warm up to her as she talked quickly and moved around the room to wake us up. She introduced herself to me as Tina. She announced that we had 15 minutes to get up, be outside our door, and line up for breakfast. Nadia got up first and changed into her clothes. It didn't take me long to get ready because all I had to do was brush my teeth. I was still wearing hospital scrubs, so there wouldn't be a change of clothes that morning.

I quickly made my bed, then Nadia and I walked out of our room and joined the line. Once everyone was in line, we made our way into the dining area. I looked at the different types of food that had been prepared. I was surprised to see so many options. We had our choice of eggs, bacon, sausage, pancakes, yogurt, or bagels. When I was at home, my normal breakfast was cereal on weekdays, and on the weekends we had some sort of eggs with sausage or bacon. I had never eaten a bagel or yogurt, so I decided to give them a shot. I was excited about trying something different. This entire experience was different, so why not?

Nadia and Megan were engaged in a conversation as I sat down at the table with them. I tried to join the conversation but was quickly distracted as the table next to us burst into laughter. I saw that Tina was at that table, and I knew that she must have done or said something funny to cause everyone to laugh so hard. As I watched them laugh, I couldn't help but smile. Nadia noticed and then leaned over to me and said, "I knew you could smile!" Her remark caught me off guard, and I immediately stopped smiling and looked around. I wasn't sure if I wanted anyone to know who I was. I didn't know how long I would be here, and I didn't trust anyone. It was a Tuesday morning and it hit me that normally at this time I would be getting ready for my first block class; instead, I was stuck in a psych hospital. My world had changed quickly, and I had no idea how things were going to turn out.

We finished breakfast and went back to our unit. Everyone went to their rooms and then lined up in front of their doors. I asked Nadia where she was going, and she said that many of the kids would be going to school. That struck me as an odd statement since we were in a hospital and I didn't think anyone could leave. She explained that there was a classroom in the hospital where we could study and focus on the assignments that were given by our schools. An instructor was present to guide us and answer questions. Hearing that made me realize that I might be in the hospital for longer than I'd thought.

As the group started to walk down the hall that led to the classroom, Tina called my name and told me I was staying back. She said that I was going to meet with Dr. Taylor. It had been less than 24 hours since I had sat in Dr. Taylor's office and learned that I would be staying in the hospital, and I felt a bit nervous as I sat down in front of her once again.

After a moment of silence, Dr. Taylor smiled and asked me how I was feeling and if I needed anything. I told her that I felt fine and that I wanted to wear my normal clothes. She said I would be able to do so in one more day. To back that up, she explained that my parents would be bringing some of my belongings as well as my schoolwork. As I processed that news, I began to wonder how long I would actually be at Richard Young. The school year had just started. It was my junior year, and I had envisioned having a great year and making more friends. This was going to mess things up, and I wondered if my friends were wondering where I was. I asked how long I was going to be in the hospital. She responded, "It depends on how, and when, you open up."

I was confused and angry, and words began to spill out of my mouth. "What did I do? I didn't do anything! Norma is the crazy one, not me!"

Dr. Taylor stayed silent as I spoke. At that moment, I felt no one was on my side, including Dr. Taylor, so I stopped talking and didn't answer any other questions. Dr. Taylor felt that was enough for that session and released me.

Tina came to the office and walked me back to the unit. I told her I needed to use the bathroom, and she allowed me to go back to my room to do so. What I really needed was to get away from everyone. I entered my room and immediately lay down on my bed. Not more than ten minutes later, Tina came bouncing into my room and happily said, "No, ma'am, it's time for you to go somewhere else!" I told her I didn't want to go anywhere. She said I didn't have a choice and got me back up on my feet.

We walked to a small room where I was given a test that involved answering questions about my feelings in different scenarios. I sat at a small table while Tina supervised me from the back of the room. My eyes began to glaze over and I felt overwhelmed as I stared at the questions. Instead of answering them, I closed my eyes and tried to drift off. That worked briefly until Tina figured out what I was doing and said, "Wake up!" There were about 200 questions, and I didn't think I would be able to answer all of them.

When I finally finished taking the test, it was time for lunch. The entire group was in the dining area when I joined them. Everyone ate and then headed back to class, with me being the exception. Tina told me she wanted me to meet her friend Mary. I figured anything would be better than sitting in a room answering questions about my feelings. We left the unit and walked farther than we had gone before. I hadn't realized how big the hospital was. We arrived at a room that looked like a classroom, and sitting at the front was a tall, slender woman with sandy blond hair. When she got up from behind the desk, I noticed that she was wearing a running suit. It turned out that she was in charge of health and fitness.

Mary asked me if I liked to exercise. I told her I liked to run and play soccer. She seemed excited to hear that I enjoyed being active. She said she walked every morning and that when I had been cleared to take part in activities, I could walk or run with her at 6 a.m. every day. I think my face revealed my uncertainty, so she added, "Or whenever you feel like it." I told her I would think about it.

As I left the room, I felt a little bit of hope knowing I could do something I liked since I was going to be locked up with no sign of leaving soon. I met up with the large group in the common space and saw Nadia. She asked what I had been up to while everyone else had been studying. I told her about the questions I had answered and how I had met Mary. It turned out that everyone was on break before heading back to class. I was introduced to the teacher who ran the classroom. He told me my schoolwork would arrive by the next day and then I could join the class.

At 3:00 p.m. study time was over and everyone met back in the unit. The group had free time before dinner. Most of the group was putting their schoolbooks away when sirens started going off. The sound made me jump, and I asked Nadia what the sirens meant. She explained that it was a signal that one of the patients was in trouble and all of the staff members would be required to assist with the situation. The sirens stopped blaring, and everyone came out of their rooms to find out what the issue was.

The sirens were for Steve, whom I had met in the small group the day before. He'd had an "episode" and was being held by several staff members who placed him in a small room that the group referred to as the "quiet room." The room was padded to keep people from harming themselves. Whoever was placed in the room stayed inside until they had calmed down. I asked if this happened often, and Nadia said not necessarily, but with Steve it did.

Dinner and the rest of the evening went by quickly. I was happy about that, because I knew that the next day I would be allowed to wear regular clothes. On Wednesday morning, I woke early and walked to the unit desk to check on my clothes. Tina was behind the desk and said she needed to check with Dr. Taylor to confirm whether it was okay. I felt deflated by her response, and I was worried that it might take even longer to get an answer. Not long after that, while I was eating breakfast, Tina walked up to me with a smile and gave me the news I wanted to hear: I could get rid of the hospital gown and put on my regular clothes. I assumed my parents had dropped off a few outfits, but I was wrong. They had brought nothing, so I had to put on the same clothes I had been wearing on the day I was admitted. I honestly didn't care what I was wearing as long as it wasn't hospital scrubs. Tina said I was likely to get more clothes by the end of the day, since I had a therapy session with Dr. Taylor and my parents that afternoon. They were also bringing my schoolbooks and my assignments.

As I thought about the afternoon session with my parents, it felt like my day had taken a turn for the worse. It had gone from a good day to a not-so-good day quickly. I didn't really want to see my parents. I didn't know what to expect from them, and I was angry that they had put me in the hospital. On the other hand, my stay at Richard Young had brought some positive changes. It was a stable and encouraging environment where I wouldn't be yelled at or hit. Instead, everyone in the hospital accepted me for who I was. I thought about how good that made me feel.

I asked Tina what time the therapy appointment was, and she said 3:00 p.m. The rest of the day I kept looking at the clock, and the time seemed to pass quickly. As 3:00 approached, I felt a pain in my stomach as well as my head. My nerves were getting to me. The time had come, and Tina came to get me. As we were walking to Dr. Taylor's office, Tina said, "Girl, you better put a smile on that beautiful face of yours." I looked up at her and told her I didn't feel very good. She asked what the problem was, and I told her that I had a headache. She said that after my meeting, she would see if I was approved to receive Tylenol for my headache.

As Tina opened the door to the office, I saw Gary and Norma sitting on the couch and Dr. Taylor in one of the chairs. I slowly walked in and sat across from the adults, making very little eye contact. Gary asked me how things were going, and I quietly said, "Just fine." Dr. Taylor started to guide the conversation after that. She asked us about things we could work on when I came back home. She also suggested how we could walk away from a tense situation and come back to discuss it calmly later. The session was calmer than I had anticipated, which reduced my anxiety a bit.

As expected, Norma and Gary had brought my clothes and schoolbooks with homework assignments. As the session ended, I said goodbye and was greeted at the door by Tina. As we walked back to the unit, she asked me how things had gone. I told her that the meeting had gone fine, but I think she could tell that seeing my parents had brought my mood down. She told me I was approved for Tylenol if I still had a headache. I said yes, since my head was still pounding. As soon as we went to the unit I went straight to my room and put my clothes away. It was nice to have something else to wear! I could feel normal and fit in with everyone else! Now I just wanted to decompress, and that is what I did as I put my head on my pillow.

M

A ROUTINE

Three weeks had passed since I was admitted to Richard Young, and my roommate Nadia and I had started to become friends. Our friendship had brought a level of trust and comfort that I had needed. Just when I felt like things had become stable, it came to an end. Nadia was informed that she was able to go home. I was very happy for her, but at the same time I was sad, too. It seemed that whenever I would get close to someone, they would be taken away. Nadia told me we would keep in touch, and she gave me her phone number and address. And with that, she went home to live her life.

Two days later, I was placed with a new roommate named Kelsey. She had been admitted due to struggles with depression and an eating disorder. During the time I had been there, I had become familiar with how things worked at Richard Young and had started making friends with the other people in my unit. I started talking to the staff and with friends. I was also getting up in the mornings and running with Mary, which felt good.

The days went by, and I found myself entering week six of my stay. I was scheduled to have another therapy session with my parents and Dr. Taylor that day, and I had learned to prepare myself before I went in. Our sessions seemed to be getting better as I felt comfortable sharing details about the physical and verbal abuse that had taken place at home. Dr. Taylor helped me to talk through things, and I felt relieved that an adult was listening to me. We were starting to figure things out, which was encouraging. During that session, Dr. Taylor told me I was going to be released from Richard Young on Friday of that week. We held our therapy sessions every Wednesday, so that meant I had two days left. I was shocked to hear that I was going home. So many emotions were going through me. I was scared, nervous, and sad at the same time. What was I going to tell my friends at school when they asked where I had been for the last six weeks?

I started to get anxious and wasn't sure I wanted to go back home. What if Norma hadn't really changed, and what if she was just putting on a show in front of Dr. Taylor? I knew one thing that would help: talking about it in the big group. After dinner the group gathered and I expressed my concerns about going home. My peers offered suggestions on how to use a few coping skills. They encouraged me with kind words and reassured me that everything would be okay.

I had never expected that I was going to be nervous about leaving Richard Young. I would never forget the day when I had entered the hospital and how much I had hated the fact that I was even there. It had become a safe place for me, and I had made friends with people who didn't judge me.

Friday came quickly, and I said my goodbyes and hugged as many people as I could. The staff members were kind to me and told me to remember what I had learned during my stay. Tina told me I was a good person and never to forget it. Gary, Norma, and I had one last session with Dr. Taylor, and then I was discharged from Richard Young. I walked out the front door and headed to the car for the first time in six weeks. We started driving away, and I nervously wondered whether things had truly changed or not.

M

DANCE

The first few weeks after I came home were calm. I started to feel like maybe we had made some progress after my stay in Richard Young. I got back into a groove with school and my friends, and I slowly started to let my guard down. Socially my friends were great, but there was one part of my social life that hadn't changed: I hadn't dated anyone yet. Throughout high school I had never had a boyfriend. It's not that I didn't want to date anyone. In middle school you typically start to have a crush, or maybe start to hang out with someone you like. That hadn't happened for me, though, and now I was in high school and it didn't feel like anything was going to change. Deep down I wished something would happen and that someone would notice me. I had many crushes, but they never became more than me admiring someone from afar.

I began to wonder if something was noticeably wrong with me. Why were boys not interested in me? My insecurities started to kick in. Was it because I was Asian? Did people know that I had trouble at home? I started hating where I was from, what I looked like, and what my home life was like. I suddenly longed to be a Caucasian girl with long blonde hair. I started to think that if I looked like that, then maybe things would be different. Maybe boys would notice me.

I had never been asked to a homecoming dance, and I wondered what it would feel like to be asked. It must be so exciting to be the center of attention and to know that someone has a crush on you! I thought about that as each dance approached.

I did have a crush on a boy named Angel during my junior year. We were just friends, and I knew that was all it ever would be, but I still had feelings toward him. Angel was in the ROTC, and every year a Military Ball was held at our high school. One was coming up, and Angel asked me if I'd go with him as his date! I was excited and said yes right away. Even though I knew he had no intention of dating me, I didn't care. I had finally been asked to go to a dance! It hadn't happened until my junior year, but I was still going! He asked me at school, and I walked on air the rest of the day.

As I left school that afternoon, I became nervous as I thought about how I was going to tell Norma and Gary. I didn't know how Norma would react, since I had never dated anyone, nor had any of my sisters. Much to my surprise, they were happy for me. Norma said we needed to find a dress. I was amazed by her reaction and suddenly filled with even more excitement. I couldn't wait! The dress that we settled on was black velvet with black-and-white checks on the bottom. I was not into fluffy, lacy, or busy types of dresses. I wanted a simple yet pretty dress.

After all the buildup, the night finally arrived. I was excited as I did my hair and got ready. Norma was adamant that I should wear a necklace with my dress, but I didn't want to. Of course she got mad at me, but I didn't care. I was going to the dance without a necklace.

Since I was the first girl in the family to go to a dance, I thought everyone would want to meet Angel. The opposite occurred. Norma and Gary never met Angel. Instead, I was dropped off at school where I would meet him prior to the dance. They didn't want us driving together to the dance.

When I arrived at school, Angel was waiting with a corsage that he pinned on me. I was finally walking into a dance! We ended up having so much fun that night! We danced and danced, and I smiled all night. Afterwards, Gary picked me up and asked how the dance had gone. I told him that I'd had a lot of fun. He told me I looked very pretty, and I was speechless. No one had ever given me a compliment like that. I just smiled and thanked him as we drove home.

When I walked into the house, Norma was waiting up and drinking her nightly hot chocolate. She asked if I'd had fun, and I told her I had. I immediately went upstairs, smiling from ear to ear. I was surprised at how nice Norma had been to me. I thought she must have gotten over the necklace incident earlier. I hadn't expected this from her.

The next week at school was great. I was excited to see Angel, and in the back of my mind I hoped that he'd had such a great time at the dance that he might want to be more than friends. Nothing had changed with our friendship, though. We remained friends, and that was it. I was still excited that we had gone to the dance together and hoped that I would get the chance again.

M

A WAY OUT

I woke up on Friday morning and grabbed a bowl of cereal for breakfast. Norma was already sitting at the table with her coffee and marmalade jelly toast. I was surprised to see her at the table because she usually didn't get up so early, and if she did, she would be just getting out of bed to see us off to school.

As I sat down with my cereal, Norma started to speak. I began to feel uneasy as she asked me about the dance that I had attended with Angel. Suddenly I realized that she was going to ask me why I had not worn the necklace that she had suggested. I couldn't believe this was happening. Norma was once again showing her true colors. She had held on to one small thing, and now she was using it to lash out at me. The dance had taken place a week earlier, and she had waited to bring this up.

I looked at her and asked, "Why are you still mad? The dance was a week ago and it's over with." My questions were all it took to send her over the edge. Her temper was so close to the surface that she had no fuse and she jumped straight to the explosion. She was standing up in an instant and had my ponytail in her clenched hand. My head snapped back, and she began screaming inches from my face.

I remembered the coping tactics that I had learned in our counseling sessions at Richard Young, and I reminded myself that I needed to stay calm so I could defuse the situation. Well, that thought came and went quickly as I reacted by shoving her away from me. I yelled, "Leave me alone!" and that angered her even more. She slapped me across the face. I quickly turned and ran past her into the living room. I grabbed my backpack and ran out the door as fast as I could.

As I ran down our street, I couldn't hold back my tears. I finally stopped at the corner and sobbed as I tried to process what had just happened. After a few minutes, I tried to pull myself together so I could continue walking to school. It didn't take long before Sarah drove up and stopped. She rolled down the window and told me to get in. I opened the car door and got in reluctantly, and as she drove, she turned up the radio so we didn't have to speak. As soon as I entered the school, I ran to the closest bathroom to splash cold water on my face in the hope that no one would be able to tell I had been crying. The school day passed quickly, and I felt a sense of dread as I thought about being at home over the weekend.

Then the dread that I was feeling shifted to anger. All of the things that my parents and I had agreed to do while we were in counseling seemed to have disappeared. The coping tactics and the calming approaches to a conversation had never happened. It had all sounded good when we were sitting together in Dr. Taylor's office. We had agreed that we would try to work together so things wouldn't get out of control.

Now it seemed like all of it had been a load of crap. They were just words that were said to make it seem like things would be okay. I decided that I wouldn't even bother trying to use coping tactics anymore. What was the point? I decided to avoid Norma, Gary, and Sarah as much as I could. After I got home from school, I went to my room and came out only when I needed to. I knew one thing for sure: I wasn't the problem—it was Norma.

Monday came, and I was informed that I would be going to a counseling session with Dr. Taylor after school. I shrugged as I walked out the door on my way to school. The more I thought about the counseling appointment, however, the better I felt. I couldn't wait to release all my anger onto Dr. Taylor and tell her how crazy Norma was. Norma and Gary picked me up after school and we headed to the appointment. I kept quiet during the drive. I looked out the window and thought, "*This is it. This is my life and I'm going to have to deal with this until I'm able to move out of the house and live on my own. I will have to deal with this bullshit for a few more years. Ugh.*"

I kept thinking about how I was going to get through things for that long. At that moment, I wished I could have called Patrick, Prudy, or even the Hinzes to come rescue me. My head was spinning and the prospect of them being a stable part of my life seemed so far away.

I opened my door as soon as we parked the car. I didn't wait for Norma and Gary as I quickly walked up to the hospital. I marched up to the counter, checked in, and sat down to wait. It didn't take long before Dr. Taylor walked into the waiting area to greet us. She asked if we were ready to talk, and before anyone could move, I stood up and said, "Can I speak to you alone, before we begin as a group?" She nodded in agreement, and we walked down the hall toward her office.

As soon as she shut her door and sat down, I immediately fell apart and started crying uncontrollably. Dr. Taylor handed me a few tissues and tried to help me calm down. After a few minutes, I had calmed down enough that I could speak. I lifted my chin and looked her in the eyes and said, "I want to kill myself, and if I have to go home after I leave this office today, I will do it."

She calmly asked me several questions about what had been going on at home. Tears kept streaming down my face as I answered her. When she was done taking notes, she picked up her phone, and the next thing I knew Tina walked into the office and was standing in front of me. I immediately started crying again, and Dr. Taylor told me to go with Tina. She told me I was being admitted and would be placed on a suicide watch. As we walked out of the office, I saw Norma and Gary sitting nearby. Norma immediately stood up and asked Dr. Taylor what was happening, but I turned away from her and kept walking. Dr. Taylor then ushered Norma and Gary into her office so she could explain that the session today had taken a dramatic turn.

Tina took me to a room where a nurse gave me hospital clothes to change into. Changing this time was different because I had to undress with the nurse and Tina in the room. Since I was on a suicide watch, all of my movements had to be observed. After I was in hospital clothes, Tina buzzed us into the unit. As I took my first steps past the doors I was filled with a sense of relief. I felt like I could breathe again. My surroundings were familiar, and I felt safe. I quickly saw friendly faces as I passed some of the counselors I had known. As I looked into the lounge area, I remembered that the hospital continually had new patients who needed help too.

I was brought to my room, and Tina let me lie down without having to join the rest of the patients. I stared at the ceiling and replayed what had just happened. I wondered what Norma and Gary were thinking. I was sure this was not the outcome they had expected when we walked in for a counseling session. The truth of the matter was that I had never intended to commit suicide. I knew that if I told Dr. Taylor I had suicidal feelings, she would have to admit me and I wouldn't have to go home with Norma and Gary.

I definitely had strong feelings and felt desperate, but I also knew that those feelings could be used to help me get away from Norma. Coming back to Richard Young the second time felt different from the first. I had more trust in the hospital and the people who were running things. I knew I was going to be safe here. I wouldn't have Norma screaming in my face, pulling my hair, or punching me. With those thoughts in mind, I knew I had to find a way to avoid ever going back to live with Norma and Gary.

M

REACHING THE BOTTOM

Two weeks passed, and I was back to the normal routine I had become accustomed to during my first hospital stay. I was running with Mary in the morning, taking a quick shower before breakfast, heading to the school room, and going to small-group sessions afterward. It was a good routine, but I knew it couldn't last forever.

Terrence, who was one of the counselors, informed me I was having a meeting the next day with my parents. I said, "Please call them Norma and Gary. They are not my parents." He told me I still needed to prepare for the meeting regardless of how I felt. I asked him how I should prepare. I had no intention of ever going back to live with them, but I didn't really know how to avoid it. He told me to write down the changes that my parents and I could work on, like how we can change the way we talk to avoid arguments, blah blah blah, the normal solutions that weren't working.

The next morning arrived, and I knew Norma and Gary were coming to see me that afternoon. A dark cloud was hanging over me. Mary asked what was wrong while we were running. I told her, and she tried to help me figure out how I was going to react to Norma and Gary. She told me to be the better person in the conversation, to be calm, and to listen. I thanked her, and we continued our run. Running and talking with Mary relieved a lot of my stress.

When afternoon rolled around, Dave came to take me to the meeting with my parents. The other counselors on staff that day reminded me to stay calm, listen, and express my feelings appropriately. I smiled and said, "Okay." When I walked into Dr. Taylor's office, Norma and Gary were already there. I made eye contact with Dr. Taylor but didn't look directly at Norma or Gary. I sat as far away from them as possible. Norma said, "Hi, there," and I didn't respond. I just looked at her without emotion.

As Dr. Taylor asked questions, Norma acted sweet and fell back on the same responses that she had given before: "I have done everything that I could do to be a good mom. Melyssa's anger issues continue to cause problems." As she spoke, Gary sat next to her silently. He looked defeated. He knew what was going on in the house, and yet he continued to let things happen. At that point I felt he was a coward. Not once had he backed me up. It was frustrating to hear Norma paint a picture in which I was the problem. I was glad that the one-on-one sessions with Dr. Taylor had allowed me to open up about each of the violent attacks that had occurred in the past. I knew Norma would deny them if I brought them up in this session. Dr. Taylor told us we needed to find some kind of solution before I could go back home. I thought to myself, "Go back?" There was no way I was going back. When I heard those words, I shut down and didn't speak for the rest of the meeting. After we were done, we scheduled another session and Dr. Taylor said, "Hopefully, in about two weeks you will be heading back home."

My heart sank as I walked out the door and found my way back to my room. I fell onto my bed with tears streaming down my face. I kept saying, "I can't go back" over and over. A cold feeling swept over me as I realized that I would rather be dead than go back to their house. This time my suicidal thoughts were real. It wasn't an act. Desperation had set in. The thought of going back home, knowing nothing had changed, pushed me over the edge. My dream of not going home had failed. No one was going to help me, including Dr. Taylor. I didn't want to go on living.

My thoughts were swirling, and I suddenly sat up. A thought had entered my mind and I immediately jumped up and started to search through my belongings. Patients in a psychiatric hospital can't have anything that they could use to harm themselves. Having a sharp item, such as a pair of scissors, would be out of the question. The sharpest item I could find was a metal hair clip. Once I found it, I went to my bathroom and shut the door quickly. I knew that for this to work, I had to slice my wrists vertically instead of going across them. I started rubbing the clip up and down on my wrist, but it was dull and wasn't having any immediate impact.

One of the counselors had been making rounds and came into my room. He knocked on the bathroom door and I told him to leave me alone. He tried to see if I would talk because he knew I was upset from the meeting, but I didn't respond. I had been leaning on the door, and now he was trying to push it open to get a look at me. I immediately pushed back, and we began to sway back and forth against both sides of the door. He quickly called out for help, and I knew I was running out of time.

I tried to scrape harder with the hair clip. If I could just push hard enough, I could cut a vein. I was bracing my legs against the sink and scraping my arm as hard as I could while sirens started to blare through the hallway. The next thing I knew, three people had pushed their way into the bathroom and grabbed me. I began screaming and kicking as I tried to push them away. They carried me out of the bathroom and more counselors grabbed my legs and arms. My wrist was bleeding, and I was trying to kick anyone that I could reach as they strapped me down. As I pulled against the restraints, I kept yelling, "I don't want to live anymore!"

After they had finished restraining me, I was carried to the padded quiet room where they finished cleaning up my wrist. After the counselors left the room, I continued to scream until I finally gave up and just cried. About thirty minutes later, Terrence, Dave, and Jeff unlocked the doors and asked me if I would stay calm if they unstrapped me. I said yes, but as soon as they did, I bolted toward the door and tried to push my way out. They wrestled me down and strapped me back down.

I realized that my attempts to hurt myself and to escape were not going to work. The hospital was designed to help me, not hurt me. I wondered what was going to happen to me. I hated my life, and now I truly didn't know what would happen next. Another hour went by, and the guys came back in and asked if I could handle being unstrapped. I said yes, again. As soon as I was unstrapped, I got up and sat in a corner and began to cry.

Dave stayed in the room to talk to me after the others left. He said, "Melyssa, you are a good person, and you should never want to end your life."

I looked at him and said, "If I ever have to go back to live with Norma and Gary again, I will kill myself. I have nothing to live for. I was taken from Patrick, I was taken from the Hinze family, Prudy was taken from me, and I have been in so many different homes where I wasn't wanted. Why would I want to live anymore?"

At that point, I was exhausted and mentally drained. It was bedtime for everyone anyway, so I was able to lie down and shut my eyes. I drifted off quickly and let the events of the day slip away.

The next morning, I had a session with Dr. Taylor. After sitting down in her office, the first thing I said was, "I can't, under any circumstance, ever live with Norma and Gary again. If I am sent back there, I will find a way to kill myself." She took notes as we continued to talk, and the session was over before I knew it. A week passed, and I was finally taken off suicide watch and allowed to wear normal clothes again.

As time passed, I continued to let everyone know that I couldn't go back to live with Norma and Gary. But even though I didn't want to live with them, I didn't know where I could go instead. I had no alternative at that point. I couldn't live at Richard Young for the rest of my teenage life, and I was too young to live on my own. As part of my therapy, I was asked to create a self-reflecting workbook about myself. I found it difficult to complete because I had no self-esteem at that point and couldn't see any good qualities in myself. As I tried to complete the workbook and thought about my future, I found myself sinking deeper and deeper into despair.

M

A GUEST

Days went by, and I continued to follow my familiar routine. Not an hour would pass when I didn't wonder what was going to happen to me. Two weeks after my suicide attempt, Tina told me that I was going to have a visitor. I instantly was overcome with dread at the thought of seeing Norma and Gary.

Tina saw the look on my face and asked what was wrong. I blurted out that I had told Dr. Taylor that I never wanted to see Gary and Norma ever again, but she hadn't listened. Tina told me that Norma and Gary weren't coming to see me; it was someone else. I couldn't believe what I had just heard. I felt so relieved. She told me the visitor would arrive in about an hour, and she said it was a man. She finished by saying that the man was a friend of my former caseworker, Prudy. I was confused because I hadn't seen Prudy in over nine years, and I didn't understand why she would be back in my life now. Did this mean that I might get placed with another family? Every time Prudy had showed up in the past, I had been moved to a new home. Was that why Prudy was getting involved?

I was nervous but eager to find out who was coming to see me. I sat anxiously at a table preparing to meet this friend of Prudy. I told myself to just listen to what he had to say. I didn't know what his intentions were, so it was hard to figure out why he was coming to visit. Deep down I had hoped that someone would take me out of this hospital and away from Norma and Gary, but I didn't know if that was possible. My thoughts ran wild as I wondered what might happen. Who would really want me at this point in my life? I had been dropped into so many different homes, and now I was a junior in high school. Anyone who wanted to adopt a child would be looking for a baby or a toddler. They would not want someone like me!

Tina told me that the man was on his way down, and she asked me to let her know if I needed her for anything. As I nodded in agreement, I started to feel a knot in my stomach and a light sweat in the palms of my hands. I looked up as the man I was meeting walked in. He was tall, had short brown hair, and was dressed stylishly. I wasn't expecting that, as Gary and Norma were not stylish at all. This guy looked younger than Norma and Gary as well. Tina came over and introduced me to Bob Brandt. As she walked away, he pulled up a chair and sat down.

Bob began by telling me that he was friends with Prudy and that she had found out I was here, and because of that she wanted him to meet me. He spoke calmly, and his tone was serious but not threatening. He came off as genuine, which made me want to listen more. He began to describe his family, and that was when things got interesting. He told me he was married and had three biological children. That was not surprising, but his next statement was. In addition to raising their three biological children, he and his wife also had adopted eight other kids! The children's ages ranged from seventeen years old down to a baby who was just a few months old. I stared at the floor and nodded as I listened to him.

Bob told me that he was an elementary school principal and that his wife Peg stayed at home with the baby. As he talked about his family, he smiled and said he was sure that I would like his kids. He asked me to tell him about my interests, and he wanted to know if I had any hobbies. At first I just shrugged and said, "Not much, really." He asked if I had played any sports, and that's when I told him that I loved soccer and that I played the flute and piccolo. He seemed interested and told me that his oldest also played the flute. I nodded in response but had nothing more to say. Our conversation lasted 40 minutes, and then he thanked me for talking with him and told me that it was nice to meet me. I looked at him and nodded as he stood up and left the room.

Immediately after Bob left, Tina came over to me with a big smile on her face and asked, "Well, how did it go?"

I looked at her and replied, "I guess good. He seemed nice, but he probably won't be back."

She asked me why I was thinking that way. "I don't know. He probably won't. I do have a question, though. Do you think I will see Prudy?"

She shrugged and said, "I'm not sure."

I was happy that Prudy knew where I was, but at the same time I was bothered that she had never returned to check on me after dropping me off at the Fliehmanns' house. I went on with my Saturday and didn't think much more about Bob and his family. I was sure he wouldn't come back, so there was no reason to get my hopes up.

As the day went on, some of my friends asked me who the guy was and if I was going to be leaving to move in with his family. I told them the same thing I had told Tina: "Nice guy, but he won't be back." I wouldn't have come back to see me either if I were him. I had hardly spoken or made eye contact with Bob. I had nothing to offer, so why would he care about me?

My friends couldn't believe that I hadn't been more open and friendly. One of them said, "Don't you want to get out of here? You should have been more friendly." I shut that down quickly by saying, "I'm too old for anyone who's looking to adopt. So why not make it easy for them to decide, and not act friendly?"

A few days later, Tina came prancing up to me with a smile on her face and shouted, "Guess what?"

I shrugged, since I had no clue.

"Mr. Bob Brandt is going to be visiting you again today!"

I couldn't believe my ears. I stared at her and asked, "Why?"

She said, "Why not?" and smiled.

"I don't know why he'd come back. I wasn't that friendly."

She laughed and said, "Well, this time, try to be a little nicer. He will be here sometime after lunch." I felt slightly confused as Tina walked away.

Lunchtime came and went, and soon I was told that Bob Brandt had arrived. I waited patiently as he was escorted into the wing. When he entered, I saw that he was not alone. Walking alongside him was a girl with long sandy blonde hair who looked to be a teenager. As they got closer, Bob said, "Hello!" and introduced me to the girl. She was his oldest daughter, Tia. It turned out that she and I were the same age, and it didn't take us long to get into a conversation. She was very nice and didn't shy away from trying to ask me questions and get to know me.

As we continued to talk, Bob got up from the table and went to talk to some of the staff members. Tia told me more about herself, and I learned that she played basketball and had a boyfriend. I was impressed that she was opening up after meeting me for the first time. I asked her if she'd like to see what my room looked like, and she said, "Of course!" We walked into my tiny room, and it didn't take long to show her the ins-and-outs of my living space. I switched gears and showed her the art project that I was working on but couldn't finish because I needed a stapler. I explained, "They won't let me have one because they don't want me to try to cut my wrists with the staples. I was on a suicide watch when I came here this time."

I had said it in a very matter-of-fact way, but I saw shock on Tia's face. I quickly realized that she wasn't used to hearing something like that from a fellow teenager. I tried to lighten the mood and suggested that we walk back to the main room.

As we were walking, I told her more about the staff. I told her about the ones I liked and the ones that I didn't. I wasn't supposed to show her my room, but I didn't care. If I was going to get in trouble, then so be it.

We sat down and then Bob came over to us and said, "Well, we are about to leave, but how would you like to get a weekend pass for next weekend? We would love it if you would come with us to a family wedding."

I just stared at both of them. I couldn't believe Bob was asking if I'd like to visit his family. He was waiting for my answer, and I quickly said, "Sure, that sounds fun!"

He smiled and said, "Great! See you next weekend."

Before they left, Bob gave me a picture of his family and told me each of their names. As I glanced at the faces of the kids in the photo I was surprised to see Caucasian, Asian, and African American kids all mixed together. It blew my mind that the Brandts had such a diverse family.

I held the photo and told Bob and Tia that I'd see them next weekend. I went to my room and stared at the photo. I started to get excited about seeing Tia and Bob again and meeting the rest of their family. Mostly, I was excited to finally get to leave for the weekend!

M

A TICKET OUT FOR A WEDDING

When I walked into the common area, my friends noticed that I looked happy and asked me what was going on. I told them I had permission to leave on a weekend pass with the family of the man who had just visited me. It felt good to see their happy reactions when I told them the news.

The next week felt like it passed slowly. I was eager to get away from the hospital, but I started getting nervous because I had nothing to wear to the wedding. Norma and Gary had only brought me a few pieces of clothing. I asked my room-mate if she had anything I could borrow, since she always looked stylish to me. We ended up putting together an outfit, and I started feeling much better.

When Saturday morning came, I got up early and waited for the Brandts to pick me up. As I waited in the common area, I saw Bob and Tia walking toward the door and got up immediately to greet them. Tia was wearing a nice sweater and a black checkered skirt that looked beautiful. Thanks to my roommate, I felt like I was dressed well and would fit in at the wedding.

We walked outside, and I saw a large van waiting for us. When I looked inside the van I saw smiling faces looking back at me. Everyone welcomed me as I climbed inside and found a spot. I felt a bit overwhelmed as everyone introduced themselves to me, but at the same time I was excited. It felt like they were genuinely happy to see me!

The plan was that we would drive to Harlan, Iowa, to attend the wedding of Bob's niece. As the van pulled out of the hospital parking lot, Tia introduced everyone a bit more thoroughly. In the very back of the van were two girls from Korea named Teresa and Terra. An Asian boy named Cody, a Caucasian boy named Tony, and a Caucasian girl named Tasha sat on the bench seat next to Tia and me. On the seat in front of us were two African American boys in child safety seats. One looked like he was possibly two, and the other was a baby. In the front passenger seat sat Mrs. Brandt, who introduced herself as Peg. She looked so pretty to me, and as she spoke her voice was calming. She seemed very kind.

The van was filled with everyone's voices as we traveled to the wedding, and I had so much fun listening to everyone talk. After we pulled up to the church, we piled out and headed inside as a group. I was introduced to quite a few people, and I was worried that people would wonder why I was there. The opposite reaction occurred, though, as everyone greeted me and made me feel welcome. No one batted an eyelash to see someone new with the Brandts. Apparently the Brandts were known for bringing kids into their household, and the amazing thing was that everyone was happy to see each of them!

I remember sticking super close to Tia and the other girls during the wedding ceremony and the reception afterwards. I had a great time, and I remember watching Teresa and Terra dance all night. The time went by quickly, and as the night was coming to an end, I started to feel sad knowing that I had to leave. It was a quiet ride back, since everyone was tired.

As I sat in the van I thought about everything that had happened. It had felt great to be able to get out of the hospital and experience something normal. I kept wishing that the night could have lasted longer. We finally pulled up to Richard Young, and the entire family said goodbye before I walked inside with Bob. He asked if I'd had a good time, and I quickly nodded and said yes. Then he said, "Maybe we can work on something for next weekend and have you spend the night at our house." I just nodded and thought there was no way I would be able to get permission for an overnight visit.

Terrence was on the night crew that evening, and he came up to greet us as we walked in. He asked how things had gone, and I said, "It was great!" with a big smile as we walked by. I went to my room and told my roommate every detail about the night. I excitedly described all the kids, the wedding, and how much fun we'd had. I told her how Bob and Peg let the kids be themselves. It was the opposite of anything I had experienced before, and I went to bed happy that night.

M

WEEKEND PASS

I got up early on Monday morning to run with Mary, and I couldn't wait to tell her about my weekend. Mary was happy for me, and she said, "It is so great to finally see you with a smile! You've got some life back in you!"

I agreed, "I'm okay."

She said, "Well, you may think you can hide your feelings, but it's written all over your face. It's okay to have different feelings. Just don't hide them. You're here to work on yourself and learn how to address how you feel with different situations."

We finished our run, and I thought a lot about what Mary had said about how I had been hiding my feelings. I had never really believed that my feelings mattered, and because of that, it seemed better to keep them inside. I had become really good at ignoring people who made me mad, and I actually had no problem dismissing them from my life forever. If they were gone, then they couldn't hurt me. At age seventeen, I felt like I had only myself to depend on. I thought I didn't need to answer to anyone, let alone share my feelings with them.

As I went to breakfast, I wondered how long I could continue to live at Richard Young. I was planning to bring up the topic in my weekly session with Dr. Taylor that day. I was also eager to tell her how my weekend had gone. As I walked into my session, she looked up and smiled, then commented, "Well, you look happy! Did you have a good weekend?" I nodded and smiled. She asked me for more details about my weekend, and of course she wanted me to tell her about my feelings. I told her they were all happy feelings until the end of the night when I had to come back to the hospital.

I asked Dr. Taylor, "How long do you think I'll have to stay here?" She looked at me without any expression on her face. My heart sank, and then she smiled and said, "What do you think about having an overnight with the Brandts this coming Friday through Sunday?" I didn't know if I had heard her right, so I repeated what she'd said and then added, "I would love that!" She stood up to end the session, saying, "Sounds great! I want you to have a good week, and I will let Mr. and Mrs. Brandt know that you are coming!"

I carried on with my usual routine during the week, but the time seemed to pass slowly. Finally it was Friday, and I felt so excited that I didn't eat anything all day! I didn't have many clothes and I didn't have a suitcase, so I just put my things in a small trash bag and I was ready to go!

When Bob arrived, I thought he would have some of the children with him. Instead, the van was empty. I started to feel nervous because I had no idea what we would talk about. As he started to drive, he did most of the talking, which made the ride to the Brandts' home in Wahoo much easier for me. I answered his questions and listened as he spoke about his family.

He told me that his wife Peg had been in a terrible car accident in December and was still recovering. They had just adopted an African American baby boy named Alex two and a half weeks prior to her accident. Peg had been driving the van with her kids in the back when a drunk driver hit them. Everyone was okay, but a piece of glass from the debris had gone through her left eye. She didn't have perfect vision in her right eye prior to that, so she had relied on the left eye to make up for it. The damage to her eye caused her to be classified as legally blind. In addition, she had broken a few ribs in the accident. Bob told me that she now had a prosthetic eye and could never drive again. *Wow!* I thought, *That is a lot to go through!* I wouldn't have known anything had been wrong, based on how she had looked and acted. He said, "She does really great, and it's nice because we live in such a small town that everyone helps everyone else."

I wondered how small Wahoo was, and it wasn't long before I found out. It literally had only one stoplight. That definitely seemed like a small town to me!

Bob had talked so much that I didn't realize we were turning into their driveway. I got out of the car and saw the house, and it seemed small for a family with eight kids. We walked to the side door, and as we were walking up the steps of the deck I saw an above-ground pool with a deck wrapped around it. It looked like it would be a fun place to hang out.

We walked into the house and were greeted by Aaron, who was about two years old, followed by Peg, who was sitting in a rocking chair feeding Alex. "Hello, Melyssa! I'm glad you are here!" Peg said. That made me feel good, and I said hello back with a smile.

Suddenly, I heard loud footsteps coming from upstairs, and then a door opened as Teresa, Terra, and Tasha came out to greet me. They told me to follow them upstairs with my bag. We went through the living room which connected to the dining room, where I noticed the baby crib for Alex. I looked at the room and noticed French doors that could close it off. It dawned on me that this was Bob and Peg's bedroom. In other words, their bedroom had been part of the dining room at one point. They were using every inch of space in their house! We went through the door and up a winding set of stairs. At the top, on the left, was a bathroom with a bedroom opposite, as well as another bedroom next to that.

Teresa, Terra, and Tasha slept in the bedroom on the left, and Tia and I would be in the other bedroom. Bunk beds helped to open the space up. We were in a finished attic. It seemed really cool to me because the walls were slanted and the rooms had character.

They had their own bathroom, and you could tell that girls were using it! There were makeup bags, curling irons, blow dryers, and Aqua Net hairspray cans everywhere. It was like nothing I had ever seen in my life, because when I lived with Norma and Gary everything was put into place and very tidy. Looking at the bathroom made me smile. I liked what I saw!

After the girls showed me around, we made our way back downstairs. By then, more kids were in the living room. Cody was now holding Alex, and Tony was lying on the floor watching TV. Each of them said hello, and the house was full of activity now. I looked outside and saw Tia getting dropped off by a guy in a blue car. She came into the house and immediately said, "Hi!" with a big smile on her face as she sat next to me.

Everyone was jabbering away as Bob came into the house with pizzas from Pizza Hut. As we all filed into the tiny kitchen to grab food, I wondered how in the world we would all fit around the table. Somehow we found spots, and before we ate the family started to pray. I was caught off guard as everyone started to say, "Bless us, O Lord, and these thy gifts, which we are about to receive..." I just stared as everyone prayed together. I hadn't been to church since I was very young and hadn't prayed before a meal. I found out they were Catholic and that they did this before every meal. It was totally new to me.

After the prayer, they started handing out pizza slices. I noticed there wasn't any meat on any of the slices; they were all cheese with various toppings. I thought it was strange but went along with it. Tia must have noticed my reaction, and she explained, "We can't eat meat on Fridays because of Lent." Teresa added, "Yes, it's this way until Easter, and then after Easter we can eat meat whenever." This was a first for me since I didn't know much about Catholic beliefs. Norma and Gary didn't attend church, but I remembered going with my other families.

Dinner ended up being fun as everyone talked and joked with each other. When we finished, they prayed again, and then everyone cleaned up. Tia asked me if I wanted to go out with her that night. All of the girls were going out with their friends but had to be back home by 11:00 p.m. to meet a curfew that Bob and Peg had set.

We went upstairs, and I watched with curiosity as the girls started getting ready. I didn't know what to do because I didn't have any makeup or different clothes to change into.

The girls were trying on each other's clothes, and they left the ones they decided not to wear on the floor. I'd have been in so much trouble if I had left my room like this at my old house! I already loved it here, and I loved these girls! They were so much fun and were living like I never had!

I ended up going out with Tia and her boyfriend that night. Wahoo is a very small town, and we drove around and met up with different groups of people who were hanging out in parking lots. It was laid back, and I had fun just going with the flow of their evening. Everyone that I met was very nice to me, and we had a lot of fun talking and getting to know each other. Before I knew it, it was time to head home so we could get there by 11:00.

We went upstairs to our rooms and rehashed the conversations from earlier. Tia said we needed to get some rest because we would be going to church in the morning. I hadn't been to a church in at least ten years, so I was eager to see what the family was used to. I drifted off to sleep feeling great about how the weekend had gone so far.

M
WAS IT A DREAM?

Morning came quickly, and we were running around with clothes and makeup as we got ready for church. It didn't seem like the girls were dressing up much, but I still didn't feel like I had many options. Luckily, Tia said I could wear something of hers. I felt like a kid in a candy shop because she had so many things to choose from. I was happy to find something to wear so I wouldn't feel out of place.

We all piled into the van and drove three minutes down the street to the Catholic church. After we walked in, we found a row that the family could all fit into. There were so many of us that we took up an entire pew. I had never been to a Catholic church before, and I started to worry that I wouldn't know what to do. I sat by Tia and Tasha, who leaned over and told me to do what they did. We immediately knelt, and they touched their foreheads, chest, and then their left and right shoulders. It was the same motion that they had used at dinner the night before when they prayed. I had seen people do it in movies, but I had never understood what it meant.

I watched and listened as the service took place. The things they said and did were memorized and had become natural for them. When it was time for them to receive Communion, Tia whispered quickly, "This time don't follow me. Just stay here." I just nodded and stayed seated. I thought that was weird because I remembered being able to take Communion at church when I lived with Shirley and Don.

The Mass soon ended, and as we walked outside, many people came up to the family to talk with them. Everyone was very friendly, and they chatted for quite a while. Then we jumped into the van and headed home to eat Sunday dinner. After changing into comfortable clothes, we went straight to the kitchen to help set the table and get dinner ready. It was like a "Sunday dinner" scene in a movie. Peg made a roast and had cooked different vegetables for side dishes. Everything was delicious and definitely beat what I was eating at the hospital!

Dinner was a fun time for me once again because I was able to get a better feel of who everyone was as they talked and joked with each other. As soon as dinner was over, we cleared the table and the kids took turns cleaning the dishes. It was an assembly line, with a few people washing and others drying.

As we finished cleaning up, Bob announced we would be leaving in 30 minutes to take me back to the hospital. I said, "Okay." I immediately felt sad inside, but I quickly smiled because I didn't want anyone to know how I felt. The half-hour flew by, and the time to leave had come.

Everyone hugged me and told me how much fun it was having me there. I just smiled at them and tried to hold back my tears. I'd had so much fun with them, and now it felt terrible to know I was heading back to the hospital.

Tia and Bob drove me back and walked in with me when we arrived. We were greeted by Dave, who checked me back in. I turned to Tia and her dad and quietly said, "Thank you for having me." Tia gave me a big smile and said, "I had so much fun!" and Bob squeezed my shoulder and said, "We will see you again soon."

I smiled and thought, "Will you?" Then I turned and followed Dave through the main door. I didn't want Bob and Tia to notice that I had tears in my eyes.

As we walked down the hallway, Dave asked if I was okay.

"Yes, I had a great time," I told him, "but I hate that I have to come back here."

He gave me a pat on the back and said he hoped things would change for me soon. I just shrugged and went to my room to unpack my bag. I stretched out on my bed and wondered if the weekend had all been a dream. The Brandt family was so fun and easygoing. Bob and Peg laughed, joked, and listened to their kids. It had been a very long time since I had been around a family like that. It was probably since I had been with the Hinze family where I had that much fun. I then started to wonder what the Hinzes were doing or what Patrick was doing. Oh, how I missed each of them and wished I could have lived with either family. They were really the last normal families I had lived with… well, in my head at least. Looking back now, the Butlers were not the norm.

I started to wonder what the rest of my life was going to be like. Would I ever leave this hospital, or would I just be put into the system and live with different foster families until I was eighteen?

THE BEST NEWS

The next day, I met Mary for our morning run and was eager to tell her about my weekend with the Brandts. She was happy for me but realized that I was also torn.

"I don't know how long I can stand being here," I said.

She encouraged me to stay positive.

"Things will work out in the way they were meant to be. I think things will turn your way," she assured me.

I nodded but still felt doubtful.

A few days later, I had my weekly session with Dr. Taylor. I told her how things had gone during my visits with the Brandts and then shared that I felt stuck. She asked me, "How would you like it if you went to live with them?"

I couldn't believe what I was hearing.

"Are you serious? I would love that!"

Then she asked if Friday would be okay. I was shocked.

"Do you mean *this* Friday?"

She smiled and said that she had talked with the Brandts earlier in the week and they had told her how well the visits had gone. "They want you out of the hospital so you can start living your life again."

I was stunned to hear those words, and I couldn't stop smiling. Dr. Taylor said she would let them know Friday worked and that I should tell my friends.

I walked out of our session and immediately went to find Tina to share my news. She gave me a big hug and told me how happy she was for me. I told each of my friends the good news as I ran into them. I don't think there was a person on the floor who didn't know!

I was walking on clouds the rest of the day as I thought about leaving Richard Young. It was Wednesday, which meant that I had one day to say goodbye to the staff and my friends.

I had thought it was going to be easy to leave, but I quickly realized how emotional it was for me. I couldn't stop crying as I talked to each staff member. They had done so much for me while I was there. They had taught me how to talk about my feelings and had built me back up. They had shown me that I was a good person and had helped me start loving who I was.

Saying goodbye is such a hard thing for me. I was happy and sad at the same time. I also was nervous about living with a new family. The Brandts said they wanted me to live with them, but three other families had told me the same thing and each one hadn't worked out. I had no guarantee that this would work out either.

On Thursday afternoon I had another nice surprise. The staff at the hospital, along with my friends who were patients, had written me goodbye notes. It made me feel so good to read each card and realize how much each of them truly cared. We all wanted each other to succeed, and those messages reminded me how much they wanted me to have a good life. My heart was full as I read the notes over and over.

With so many thoughts and emotions swirling around in my head, I couldn't sleep that night as I kept trying to picture how my life was about to change.

M

HERE WE GO

Friday morning came, and I was able to do a final run with Mary. It was great seeing her one more time. I had loved my morning runs with her and I would miss them. As we talked, she told me to remember what I had learned and not to shut people out so quickly. I thanked her and told her how much our runs had meant to me. Running had helped me to release my stress, and ever since then I've leaned on it when I needed an outlet.

I went to breakfast, but I wasn't hungry. I had butterflies and I knew Bob would come soon to pick me up. Packing my personal items was easy. I only had a small box of belongings to bring with me. Norma and Gary had refused to bring anything more than a few pieces of clothing. I had nothing from my past to show who I was.

Bob arrived, and I met him at the front entrance. Tina brought me to meet him, and she gave me a long hug and whispered, "You are special, and I will miss you."

I started crying. Then I was upset because I didn't want Bob to think I was crying because I didn't want to live with his family. We finished our goodbyes and then headed to Wahoo, the place I was going to call home.

The car drive went well because Bob did all the talking. He spoke about everyone in the family and filled me in on what each of the kids were doing. He had to drop me off at their home with Peg because he needed to get back to work. Peg was home with Aaron and Alex, and they were planning to go to the high school track meet not long after I arrived.

As we entered the house, Peg welcomed me and let me know that I could take my belongings upstairs to the room where I had slept the previous weekend. I went up and set the box on my bed and then came back downstairs. Peg was folding laundry, and she made small talk with me while Aaron played with his toys. He showed me each of his toys, which was fun and kept me busy. It was easier having Aaron there to keep us preoccupied.

When we were talking and I said "Mrs. Brandt," she mentioned that I could call her "Peg" if I wanted to, or even "Mom." I thought about it and decided to call her Peg but not Mom.

Before too long we were picked up by one of Peg's friends to go to the track meet since Peg couldn't drive.

At the high school we watched Teresa, Tasha, and Terra run. As we were sitting in the stands, Tia ran up to say hello. I was glad to see her and immediately felt some of my anxiety go away.

After the track meet ended, we went home where all the kids had gathered. They were all so welcoming! It felt good! We ate and then the girls got up quickly as they had plans to go out that night. Tasha told me that I could hang out with her since Tia and Teresa would be with their boyfriends and Terra had plans with her friends. I was excited to go out with Tasha.

Tasha was a year younger than I was, and she was one of the Brandt's biological children. She was athletic, had long blonde hair, and had a great sense of humor. What I didn't know then was that Tasha and I would end up going out many more times and having A LOT of fun together!

Our usual Friday and Saturday nights consisted of driving around town and meeting people in parking lots. Hey, anything was better than what I had been doing at the hospital, so that was fun for me! I met new people that weekend and had fun fitting in with Tasha.

The weekend soon ended, and I got ready to begin school. I didn't have a schedule yet, so I went to classes with Tia at first. Wahoo Neumann was a very small Catholic school. There were probably 45 kids in the entire junior class, and everyone knew everyone else, including all the kids in the other grades. We had to wear uniforms that consisted of a white or navy polo shirt and navy pants. Coming from a large school like Bellevue East with hundreds of kids in each class and no dress code, this was a big change for me.

The teachers knew who everyone was, especially the Brandt kids. Peg had once worked at the high school, and Bob was the elementary school principal. During passing periods I would see the other girls from home in the hallways. I remember Teresa yelling, "Hey there, sister!" as we saw each other. It caught me off guard to realize that she already considered me her sister, even though I had only been there for three days! I just smiled and waved at her and kept taking things in. I felt like I had been dropped into a new life, filled with new family members and places, and I suddenly had to adjust and accept where I was. So far, so good, but it felt slightly overwhelming to adjust so quickly.

M

ICE CREAM BREAK

As I continued to shadow Tia, she told me that the following day we would be staying after school because we needed to do our "conditioning." I asked her what conditioning was, and she said that if you didn't participate in a sport for school, you had to do conditioning, which consisted of running. I was fine with that since I liked running.

The next day after our last class we changed into our work-out clothes for conditioning. The goal was to run one mile that day. There were about six girls in our group. Our route would begin at the school, go through part of the town, and then end up at school again.

We started our run, but as we made our way through Wahoo, we noticed that the ice cream store was on our route. This proved to be too tempting to resist, so we gave in and stopped for a treat. Our running times were going to be a bit longer that day! Our plan had been going great, but apparently we were seen by one of the teachers who then reported us to Father O'Byrne, who coached track, cross country, and conditioning.

When we got back from our run, Father O'Byrne already knew what we had done. As we ran up, he started yelling at us in his thick Irish accent, "Get up against the wall!" As he was scolding us about how we shouldn't have stopped for ice cream, I started yelling back at him in an attempt to explain. Tia quickly covered my mouth with her hand, leaned over, and said, "We are in the wrong, so be quiet!" The more I tried to talk, the angrier he got, so I just stopped talking. Tia told me that we shouldn't ever yell at an adult.

After Father O'Byrne scolded us, we were excused for the day. I thought for sure we would be in trouble when we got home, but nothing was said about the incident. I couldn't believe it. Either Bob and Peg didn't know what we had done, or they realized we had already been scolded. In the past, I would have been yelled at or worse. I did learn something that day, though. Tia showed me that I didn't always have to push back and that I needed to learn how to stay calm in some confrontations.

As I got into my classes, I started making friends and found an opportunity to do something I loved. I could take part in the marching band again! To my surprise several of the kids in the family were also in the band. I played the flute and piccolo, Tia played the flute as well as the drums, Tasha played clarinet, Teresa played the drums, and Terra played the flute and piccolo.

When I had been part of the Bellevue East band, it was an amazing experience! We had a huge band and won many competitions through the years. I quickly realized that Wahoo Neumann's band was nowhere near the size of Bellevue East's band, but I kept an open mind. The band teacher, Mrs. Couton, was very nice, and I could tell she loved directing the band. At first, I was disappointed because we were not even close to what I was used to, but I thought maybe I could give a few tips about what I had learned in the past when I got used to Mrs. Couton. I didn't want to start off on the wrong foot as I had done with Father O'Byrne, so I went along with things. I had to borrow a flute because my flute had been left behind at the house in Bellevue. I was hoping that I could get it from Norma and Gary at some point. It was an open-hole flute that was pretty awesome, and I loved it.

Between running and band I had found two of my favorite outlets. It felt like things were falling into place, and I was relieved.

M

"NO COMPRENDE"

I gradually started feeling more relaxed after arriving at the Brandts', but I still had a lot of pent-up anger. Sometimes the tiniest thing would set me off, and I wasn't sure why. My anger would show up in different ways and in different intensities.

One of the classes on my school schedule was a Spanish class taught by Sister Maria, a short Hispanic nun who talked a lot. One day she struck a nerve when she said something that felt like it was directed at me. It wasn't meant to be a personal attack, but for some reason I took it that way. I felt my heart beating faster as my anger rose quickly, and I reacted by yelling, "Fuck you!" at her.

The classroom quickly went silent. Sister Maria and I stared at each other without saying a word, and then I was literally saved by the bell. Everyone got up and I quickly gathered my things and left the classroom. Spanish was my last class of the day, and as I walked down the hall, I saw Sister Maria heading into the office. I was sure that she was going to call the Brandts to let them know what had happened.

As I left the school building, I met up with Tia and told her the story. As she listened to what I had said to Sister Maria, she just stared at me in disbelief.

"Why would you do that?"

I looked away and said, "She made me mad."

Tia was speechless. We walked to the after-school conditioning program, and I wondered how things would be when we got back home. I was pretty sure that I was going to be in trouble when I got there. I started to think negatively about myself and my actions, and a thought crept into my mind: "They will probably get rid of me sooner or later because I screwed up."

When we got home that night, Bob was there when I walked in. Here it was. Time to face the music.

"I heard you and Sister Maria had a problem today in Spanish class today," he said.

I looked at him and finally found my voice: "She made me mad."

He calmly said, "Well, let's try not to drop the F-bomb again."

I nodded and said, "Okay."

That was the end of the discussion. I couldn't believe it. I had thought for sure he'd yell at me, but he didn't. Why was he so calm when he talked to me about it? The school had called and told him what I had done. He had every right to be angry, yet he talked to me calmly and trusted that I wouldn't do it again. His response was the opposite of what I had been used to. It showed me so much about him. I had made a mistake, but he still believed in me.

I felt a sense of calm wash over me as I walked upstairs to talk to the girls. They had questions for me, and I explained everything. After we talked, I realized that they knew I had messed up, but they also supported me when I said that I wouldn't do it again. When I went back to school, I dreaded going back to Spanish class and seeing Sister Maria. To my surprise, she treated me just like everybody else had. She acted like things were normal, and we ended up getting along during the rest of the school year. Moments like these continued to leave lasting impressions on me.

M

PEG

As school was winding down in May, we came home to find out that Peg had to go to Boston for surgery because she had broken her leg. Peg had Gaucher disease, a condition that causes fatty substances to build up in certain organs, particularly the spleen and liver. The organs enlarge and can malfunction. The fatty substances also can build up in bone tissue, weakening the bone and increasing the risk of fractures. Peg could be having a normal day and, in an instant, an accidental bump could result in a broken bone. That was exactly what had happened this time. Since Bob and Peg had to leave for a while, Bob asked his brother to come over and stay with us.

Bob's youngest brother, Ted, was now in charge of all seven kids. He came by himself, while his wife Deb stayed in Kearney to watch over their own children. Thank goodness he had some experience with kids! Ted was a jovial guy, very easygoing, with a great personality. We didn't know how long he would be staying with us, and luckily, we all had regular routines.

As each day passed, I thought about Peg and wondered how she was doing. I wanted things to go well so she could heal quickly. She had been through so much. She was dealing with this disease after recovering from the car accident that had left her legally blind, all while taking care of seven kids! I couldn't imagine what she was going through. Ted would give us updates each day and then let us do whatever we wanted. He never really questioned where we were going or what we were doing. Again, I was not used to being trusted in that way. Norma had always wanted to know who I was with and what I was doing. I was rarely allowed to go out.

We had so much fun with Ted, and we gave him the nick-name "Uncle Buck" because we loved that movie! I'm not sure Ted liked his new nickname, but he still laughs whenever we bring it up to this day. Ted stayed with us for an extended weekend, and then friends and teachers came to the house to watch us until Bob and Peg came back from Boston.

I thought it was amazing that the Brandts had so many friends who were willing to help their family. I had never seen that kind of support from a community. There had been times when Norma had been in the hospital for several days, and once for several weeks, yet nobody had come over to help us. Looking back, I think support from friends says a lot about the relationships a family builds.

As school ended and summer vacation began, Bob and Peg returned from Boston. The surgery had gone well, and now Peg needed to rest and recover. Once again, their friends showed up to help with meals or to watch Aaron and Alex since they were so young. It all left a huge impression upon me. I hoped that one day I would make friends who cared enough to help me get through tough times.

M

WORKING AWAY

Each of the girls in the family had a job where she earned her own spending money. I couldn't wait to be able to do the same thing. The girls told me that I could make some good money close to the end of the summer by detasseling corn. We lived in a rural area that was close to several farms, so there were plenty of opportunities for detasseling. Each year the kids did it and seemed to earn a fair amount of money. I had no idea what was involved, but it sounded like it would help me towards my goal.

Before detasseling began, I applied for a position at the Civic Center, which was a local recreational center. I ended up getting the position, which involved taking on several roles. I would be greeting people at the front desk and checking them in, running the scoreboard during basketball games, working in the concession stand during the baseball games, and even being a line umpire for baseball games (one of my least favorite responsibilities).

Regardless of the work I did at the Civic Center, I loved the job because it allowed me to meet a lot of people. They knew right off the bat that I was a "Brandt." I technically wasn't, though. I was just living with them, and I wasn't sure what was going to happen in the future. Things had been going well, but I wouldn't allow myself to get too comfortable. It had only been a few months, and they could still find a reason to ship me off if they wanted to. That was my mindset, and I truly believed it. At that point in my life, how could I not? For the moment, though, I told myself to go with the flow and see if things would continue to get better.

At the Civic Center I worked with a girl who attended the other high school in town. Her name was Kari, and I had seen her a few times when we had gone out on the weekend. I knew she had a lot of friends at school, but I thought we would never be friends because she was in the "popular crowd" and I didn't feel like I was close to that.

Kari and I often had front desk duty together, and we ended up having a lot of fun. One night she asked me if I had any plans after work. I had nothing planned, since Tia and Tasha were both going out with their boyfriends. Kari asked if I'd like to hang out. I said I'd love to. She told me she would pick me up and we'd find something to do. I was so excited that someone wanted to do something with me!

Tia picked me up from work that day, and I told her that Kari had invited me to hang out with her. Tia smiled and said, "That's awesome. Kari is a nice girl!" I asked Tia if she thought it would be okay with her parents if I went out with a friend, since I had never really gone out with anyone besides the Brandt girls. She didn't hesitate: "Of course! Just tell my parents."

During dinner Bob asked us what our plans for the night were. Everyone piped in to let him know what they were doing, and then I told him about Kari asking me to hang out. He gave a simple response: "Okay, sounds great! Have fun!" I was blown away. He didn't ask where we were going or what we were doing. He just told us to be back by curfew, which was 11:00 p.m., and to let them know when we were home. We quickly finished up at the table and then ran upstairs to get ready. This was one of the best parts of being together. All of us girls would be upstairs getting ready to go out, dancing to music, and laughing. It was how I had pictured college might be like if I ever went.

Kari picked me up that night, and we rode around town, stopping periodically to talk to different groups of friends. She knew a lot of people from the Wahoo public high school, and I knew several people from Wahoo Neumann Catholic high school. We would hang out with each group, and it ended up being a lot of fun. I was able to meet even more kids my age, which meant a lot.

Riding around may not sound exciting, but you must remember this was a small town, and it was a way for kids to get out and socialize. When the night ended, Kari dropped me off and I went inside to tell Bob and Peg I was back on time. I went upstairs to find Teresa and Terra, and not long after came Tia and Tasha. We sat and talked about our nights, and I told them how much fun I'd had with Kari. I enjoyed hearing their stories and realizing that my story fit in with theirs. It made me feel like I belonged. At times it was hard to believe that I could feel this way. "This is what sisters do," I thought, "and now I'm right there with them."

M

MOVING ON UP

As summer rolled along, I kept busy with my job as well as hanging out with Kari. She and I became inseparable, and I considered her my best friend. Everyone else in the house was busy with jobs, friends, and having fun in the summer. Peg had continued to heal from her injury, and things in the house felt like they were going great.

One day Bob and Peg called us all into the living room for a family meeting before everyone headed out. As everyone sat down, I started to feel nervous. Were they going to make some changes with the kids? Was this where they were going to tell me that things weren't working out with me, and they had found another family for me? These nervous feelings were common for me. It was a defense mechanism that would kick in quickly.

To my surprise, Bob and Peg told us they had bought a house down the road from us. We were all speechless. Bob explained that the other house was much bigger and would be better for Peg in the long run because it was wheelchair accessible. Over time her bone disease could put her in a wheelchair, and they wanted to think ahead and prepare.

It sounded exciting; however, we suddenly had a big concern. We loved having a swimming pool at our house! Bob and Peg laughed and told us to come with them to visit the new house. We all piled into the van, and Bob drove two minutes up the street to a huge brick house with a long driveway. We quickly ran inside to check it out.

As soon as we walked in, we saw a big living room that led to a huge kitchen that looked out over an in-ground swimming pool with a diving board. Our potential disaster had been averted! Swimming at home would still be an option!

We ran through the rest of the house to see how things were laid out. There were three bedrooms upstairs and a huge unfinished basement with one bedroom already built out. Bob and Peg said that they were having two more bedrooms built in the basement, as well as a bathroom. Even with the new rooms, the basement would still be big enough that we could have a hang-out area with furniture and a TV.

The new house seemed like a mansion compared to the current house. We would have so much more space. We kept walking around the house in amazement!

We couldn't wait to begin moving. Bob mentioned that the move wouldn't take place for a few weeks because they wanted the bedrooms and bathroom in the basement to be finished first. While we were waiting to move, we could pack up our things and get ready.

In my case, packing wouldn't take long because I had brought very little when I moved in with the Brandts. I still didn't have any of my belongings from the past—nothing that would show where I had been. I had no photos that could tell part of my story. I didn't have books or keepsakes or anything that was personal. I had a small box of clothes and the pink cat that my aunt had given me when I lived with the Butlers. That cat will always be with me because it connects me to my past. I will never part with it.

Over the next few weeks, everyone packed up their belongings, worked at their jobs, and spent time in the pool. Moving day finally came, and everyone was eager to get into the new house. As we settled in, we had fun helping each other get our rooms situated. We had the entire downstairs to make our own. It was awesome! We couldn't wait to have our friends over to swim in the pool and just hang out. As we settled in, that is exactly what we did.

I became very excited when Bob shared that Prudy was going to be coming to the new house to see how things were going for me. After her first visit, she visited me every other month and occasionally brought another caseworker with her. I loved the fact that the Brandts allowed her to visit me. At the end of each visit, Prudy would always ask me if I needed anything, and I would request certain things.

During Prudy's first visit, for example, I asked if she would go to Norma and Gary's and get my photo albums from when I had lived with the Butlers. I also asked for the rest of my clothes as well as my flute. I had an amazing open-hole flute, and I wanted to play it in the band during the school year. Prudy said she would check with Norma and Gary about picking up my things.

A few weeks went by, and Bob asked what I thought about Gary coming out to the house to visit me. I didn't really want to see Gary, and I definitely didn't want to see Norma. I told Bob I only wanted to see Gary if he brought me my flute, pictures, and clothes. Then I waited and hoped that my requests would be granted.

M

WHERE IS MY FLUTE?

Summer would be coming to an end soon, and we would start practicing for fall sports. Before school began, we spent a few weeks detasseling corn. Each morning we would get up very early to ride in a bus to the cornfields. We would walk down each row and remove the tassels from the tops of the cornstalks. The weather was extremely hot and humid, and we ended up with mud all over us. On top of that, we had to wear long sleeves and jeans with a trash bag over our clothes to prevent the corn husks from cutting us.

Detasseling was hard, but the girls had been right when they said we could earn good money. We could get paid by the row or by the hour. Tasha and I chose to be paid by the hour and the other girls chose to be paid by the row because they were much faster than we were. Most of the kids in Wahoo detasseled corn, so this gave me another opportunity to get acquainted.

Tasha, I, and a few other girls would detassel most of our row and then walk to the end, sit down, and talk while we waited for the boys to finish the rest of our rows. We would jump up as soon as we heard them coming and act like we had been detasseling the whole time. We thought we were pretty funny!

We were usually in the field until 11 a.m. or noon, and then we would all pile into the bus and ride home. After we got home, we would rush in to take showers, and then rest up because we had sports tryouts for high school. Thank goodness detasseling lasted only a few weeks! When high school sports two-a-day practices began, we were done detasseling!

Tia and Terra were going to try out for volleyball, and Tasha and Teresa were planning to try out for cross country. I didn't know what sport I wanted to play, so I decided to follow Tia's example and try out for volleyball. I had played in junior high, but I'm pretty sure everyone made the team back then.

Volleyball started with a practice session that led to the tryout. I was relieved that Kari and Tia were there, because I wasn't familiar with the other girls. I noticed right away that the girls who tried out were good athletes. I felt like I was just okay in comparison, but I still hoped to make the team.

After the tryout, we were told that we would find out who made the team in a few days. I knew Tia and Kari would make it, but I wasn't so sure that I would. A day later we were home preparing food for dinner when Bob came inside and asked me how I was doing. I said that I felt good. He then mentioned that he had been talking to the volleyball coach earlier, and she thought it would probably be better if I went out for cross country instead of volleyball. Before I could say anything, Tasha screamed out, "Yes! You will have fun in cross country!" I just looked at her as I tried to process what Bob had just said.

I had run cross country at Bellevue East and felt like I was just average, but I told Bob that it sounded good and that I would give it a shot. As I thought about it, I felt a bit nervous because the coach was Father O'Byrne, and he was the teacher that I had sassed off to the previous year when he scolded us for eating ice cream instead of running.

It was nice of the volleyball coach to tell Bob that I wasn't going to make the team. It was hard hearing the news, but it didn't come as a surprise. I knew that I wasn't very good at volleyball.

The next morning, we headed to school where Tia and Terra went off to volleyball practice, and Tasha, Teresa, and I went to cross-country practice.

It turned out that my nervous feelings about cross country had been unfounded. All of the girls on the team were nice to me, and Father O'Byrne treated me well. It was as if the ice cream incident had never happened! He was a great coach who pushed all of us to do our best.

I wasn't very fast and I knew I'd never make the varsity team, but I didn't care. I just enjoyed being on a team with so many nice girls. In addition, running helped me to clear my mind.

In addition to getting involved in cross country, I wanted to participate in the band again. One question occupied my mind: Where was my flute? I asked Bob whether he had heard any updates about my flute, and he said he would call Prudy to find out. I was adamant that I needed my flute before school started. A few hours later, Bob told me he was planning to go to the police station where Gary worked so he could pick up my flute. A few days later, we made a plan that Bob would pick me up at school after getting my belongings from Gary. I was looking forward to having some of my things back.

When I got into the car, I immediately asked for my flute. Bob nodded and said that it was in the back seat. I reached back quickly to get it and as I did, I noticed that the case looked different. I opened it up and looked down at an old, slightly bent flute. I immediately started yelling, "What is this? This isn't my flute!"

Bob looked at me and said, "That is what Gary gave me." I was furious! I kept saying, "This isn't my flute!" I then asked if Gary had brought my photo albums and clothes. Bob said that Gary had only given him the flute case.

I was so angry that all I could do was yell and cry. When we got home, I immediately jumped out of the car and went straight to my bedroom. Not long after that, Tia came down and tried to talk to me. I was so angry that no one could have made me feel better about anything. She soon left me alone, and Bob came down to try and talk with me. I remember telling him how much I hated Gary and Norma and saying that they had no right to keep my things. I barely had anything that would show who I was. I had been bounced between homes multiple times, and now that I had found a family that cared about me, I still couldn't escape the control that Norma had over me. Why would she keep my belongings if she truly didn't care about me?

I felt defeated and angry. Bob just let me yell, cry, and carry on. He waited until I calmed down, and then we started to talk a bit more. He reminded me that there are things that we can control and things that we can't.

"We have to keep moving in the right direction," he said. "I'm sorry this happened, but I promise that you will have a flute to play this year. It won't be your old one, but it will work."

Bob was always able to find a way to smooth things over and to make me feel better. He finished by saying, "School starts on Monday. Are you going to let this one thing ruin band for you?"

I just looked at the floor and shrugged. It always took some effort to get over my anger, but he had helped to push me in the right direction. It was a reminder that Bob's good actions could help to overcome the effects of someone else's bad actions—yet another great lesson.

M

BRANDT ADDITIONS

I soon realized living with the Brandts was awesome, and I felt like I never wanted to leave. I was afraid to let them know that, though, because whenever things had started going smoothly for me in the past, everything had fallen apart. I decided that I needed to protect my heart and not let people break it anymore.

I still wouldn't address Bob and Peg as Mom and Dad. I really didn't use their names much, either. I would just walk up to them and start talking. The Brandts were very patient with me. I went through my share of ups and downs at first, but with the help of the Brandt kids and my conversations with Bob and Peg, I was learning to find my way. Prudy continued to visit, and I realized that she wanted to make sure she stayed in my life.

I had been with the Brandts for about six months when I came home one day and a girl who was pregnant was sitting in the living room. We were told that she was going to live with us until she had her baby. She was considering putting her baby up for adoption. I thought the Brandts were awesome to let a random pregnant girl live with them until she had her baby. I had never been around anyone who was so kind.

The girl's name was Carrie, and she didn't seem interested in talking with us. When Bob said, "I like your sweater," her response was a sharp, "What's it to you?" I couldn't believe she'd said that, but I told her, "You may not like it here at first, but in the end, you won't want to leave."

Over the next year, several other pregnant girls moved in with us until they had their babies, after which they placed them for adoption and went back to their families. Most of the girls stayed in contact with the Brandts over the years, which showed the impact that the family had on them.

When fall came around, the Brandt family grew yet again. Bob and Peg decided to adopt two siblings, a brother and sister named Nick and Leigha who were toddlers at the time. In addition, we also gained another high schooler named Brenda. The Brandts' house was full again!

Throughout all of these changes, I continued to find my place in the family. I got the nickname Mel thanks to Aaron. He had trouble saying my name, so he called me Mel and it stuck with me. All of my friends and family called me Mel from that point on. Hey, when you get a nickname, you know that you are really fitting in!

M

AN UNEXPECTED MEETING

Thanksgiving was a huge deal in our house. All of the aunts, uncles, and cousins would come over, and the house would be packed to the rafters. It was a blast, with conversations happening all over and kids running in every direction!

Christmas was equally important, and it was always centered around our church. The Christmas Eve service was beautiful, and I was becoming more familiar with the Catholic Mass. It was starting to feel much more comfortable to me.

Christmas Day was always fun with all the excitement around gift giving. It meant a lot to me when Peg knitted a stocking with my name on it. Each of the kids had a stocking with their name on it, and seeing one with my name felt like closure for me. It meant I wasn't going to be sent away. The Brandts were my family now.

As we continued to attend church and I saw how much the family relied on their faith, it made an impression on me. After thinking about it for quite a while, I decided I wanted to become Catholic just like everyone else in the family. I asked

Peg what I had to do to become Catholic, and she said that we needed to find out whether I had ever been baptized. I would then go through classes, and at Easter I would be confirmed.

I was super excited! Peg asked me if I knew what church I had been baptized in and if I had a baptismal certificate. I told her we needed to contact the Butlers to find out if I had been baptized. I mentioned that I knew their phone number because I had memorized it.

I had never told anyone about it, but I used to call the Butlers' phone number sometimes and then hang up when someone answered. I never had the guts to say anything. I just wanted to hear their voices. Beth or Earl usually answered the phone, but never Patrick. I always wondered if I would have the courage to say something if Patrick answered, but I never had the chance to find out.

In addition to calling the Butlers and hoping to connect with Patrick, I had taken it a step further with Tia's help. One time we were driving into Omaha, and I gave her directions to a certain neighborhood. We ended up stopping on a street, and I stared intently at one house. I told Tia to ring the doorbell of the house and then come back to the car. Tia asked me, "Whose house is this?" I told her it was the Butlers' house and that I just wanted to see someone.

"No way am I ringing the doorbell," Tia said. "What if they see us? What are we going to do?"

I said, "We can drive off. I just want to see what they look like now."

We didn't end up ringing the doorbell after all, but we did sit in front of their house for a while as I waited for someone to walk out the front door.

I hadn't told anyone about those things, but now here we were, ready to pick up the phone and talk to the Butlers after all. When I told Peg that I had memorized the Butlers' phone number, she said, "Well, we will call them and find out if you were baptized."

Peg made the call as I was in the other room on a different phone listening in. Beth answered, and Peg did all the talking. She told Beth who she was and why she was calling. I eagerly listened and couldn't believe we were doing this. I could hear someone else also picking up another phone to listen, and they exclaimed, "It's our Melyssa on the phone!"

The good news was that we were able to confirm what I had thought: I had been baptized. The Butlers were so excited that they asked if they could come and see me. We ended up scheduling a day when they could come out to our house.

I learned years later that when Peg called the Butlers to find out if I had been baptized, it had struck a nerve when she'd heard someone say, "It's our Melyssa." Bob and Peg had worked hard to help every child who entered their home. They considered each of the kids their own. Peg told me that she had wanted to say, "Wrong! She is now *my* Melyssa!"

Both Bob and Peg viewed me as their own child, and I loved them for that. I also appreciated that they were always so open for any of us adopted kids to find, meet, and spend time with our biological or previous adoptive family members. Aaron, my younger brother, had a great relationship with his birth mom and grandmother. We saw them all the time, and they were considered family. Teresa and Terra had found their dad and siblings years earlier. They decided to spend Thanksgiving with their birth family the year they reconnected, and Bob and Peg supported their decision. Alex also reconnected with his birth family, as did Nick and Leigha.

Bob and Peg never felt threatened by any of our birth families or adopted families from the past; they just continued to show us love and support.

I became very excited when I thought that maybe I would be in contact with the Butlers again and get to see Patrick.

I now had a date scheduled and could get ready to meet with the Butlers. Bob and Peg asked if I wanted them to be in the room with me, and I said, "Absolutely. I want you there, and I definitely want Tia to be there too!"

I had a few weeks to gather my thoughts and put together a list of questions that I wanted answers to. Mostly, I couldn't wait to see Patrick again!

The days seemed to speed by, and I was getting more and more anxious. Tia walked into my room and asked me if I was nervous. I said, "Very. Promise not to leave me alone with them." She nodded and promised to stay with me.

The night before the meeting, I had trouble sleeping. I wondered what the Butlers looked like now, what their life was like, and whether they ever missed me.

Morning came fast, and I dressed quickly. I could hardly eat my breakfast because my stomach was in knots. It had been eleven years since I had last seen them. I kept wondering how things would play out.

Bob and Peg were very supportive and reassured me that everything would be okay.

When the time came, I heard the doorbell ring but I couldn't get up to open the door. I just sat and stared at the door. Bob realized that I wasn't going to move, so he went to the door and let them in. He introduced himself and Peg and Tia, and then I slowly walked into the living room. I was so nervous that I just stood in place and smiled.

Dere, the Butlers' youngest daughter, walked over and gave me a hug. She had been a toddler when she had last seen me, and I barely recognized her. We all sat down and stared at each other. As I looked at them, I suddenly realized that Patrick wasn't there. My heart sank when they told me that he couldn't make it. I wondered why he hadn't come. Did he not know that they were coming to see me? Or did he know and not want to see me? I didn't get an answer because I didn't feel comfortable asking them at the time. The whole situation felt strange. I found out later that Earl and Beth had not told Patrick that they were coming to see me.

My thoughts were interrupted by the small talk that was taking place. It didn't last long, and then the room became extremely quiet. Earl finally broke the silence by asking me if I had any questions. Before I could answer, Dere blurted out, "Yeah, Dad, why did you guys dump her?"

I looked at them in shock. The room was silent. I hadn't expected to hear that question, but truth be told, I wanted to hear the answer.

Earl and Beth just looked at each other, and finally Earl said, "It was the best thing to do because you and your mom just didn't bond." I looked at the floor as I tried to process what he had said.

Peg and Bob then started to tell them what activities I was involved in at school. They told them about my job and mentioned that I was going to graduate soon and go to college. They were able to lighten the mood in the room, and I was so grateful for their help. They always knew exactly what to do.

I finally asked them how my cousin Corey was doing. Corey, Patrick, and I had been inseparable as kids. We did everything together. Corey was the son of Beth's sister Kate. I told them that I still had the pink cat that Aunt Kate had given me. I had grabbed that pink cat when I thought I would be leaving for a while. It was the only thing I still had from my time with the Butler family, and I had taken it with me everywhere. They smiled as I said that, but they didn't say anything in return.

I went on to tell them that the last family I had been with had kept all of my baby pictures and that they hadn't give them to me when I moved in with the Brandts.

"When I moved here, I had a box of clothes and my cat," I said. "That was it."

The room was silent again after I had finished talking. When Earl and Beth realized that I had moved to different homes after leaving them, I think they were unsure how to respond.

Earl finally spoke up and answered my question. "Corey is still in Omaha and lives with his mom, as well as Beth's mom. Nan, his grandma, lives in a furnished apartment in the basement of Kate's house."

I was excited to hear about Corey, and I quickly asked if I could have his phone number. They didn't have a problem with it and wrote the number down for me. It was a start. At least I would be able to connect with a cousin who was my age. I couldn't wait to call him!

As we were wrapping up the visit, Earl asked if they could come to my graduation. I looked at Bob and Peg for guidance, and Bob said, "That is up to Melyssa." I looked back at Earl and said, "Sure, you are welcome to come." I wasn't going to say no because I didn't want to hurt their feelings. As I answered him, I wondered if we would ever be able to fix our relationship. I was so hurt by what they had done, but I also loved them so much. I had mixed feelings about everything that had happened.

They got ready to leave, and Earl and Dere gave me a hug. Beth followed them and gave me a short, awkward hug. It felt strained, but I hadn't expected much more than that.

After they left, I was relieved that the meeting had gone somewhat smoothly. Peg, Bob, and Tia asked me how I was feeling. I told them I was fine but I felt disappointed that I didn't get to see Patrick. I told them I couldn't wait to call Corey.

Not long after that, all the other kids came home and asked me how my visit with the Butlers had gone. They all knew what it meant and were anxious to see how I felt about it. I loved the fact that everyone cared so much about me.

After talking with everyone, I went downstairs to have some time alone. I replayed the meeting several times in my head and thought about what was said. I was trying to process what had happened. And then without warning, I started crying. I wasn't sure why at first. Everything just started to rise to the surface, and the emotions brought tears.

As I continued to cry, I suddenly felt angry. Questions raced through my head. How could they have done what they did? Are they still a happy family without me? I felt like I should still be with them, and I wasn't! I cried into my pillow and then tried to calm down.

Soon, Bob came downstairs to check on me. He knocked on the door and then came and sat on my bed. I told him that I didn't want to talk, and then I started crying again. Bob sat with me and just let me cry. When the tears stopped, I told him what I was feeling. He listened and reassured me that it was okay to have those feelings and that I shouldn't keep them bottled up.

"You are a good kid, and you did nothing wrong," he said.

I just stared at the ground as I listened to him.

Bob also told me I didn't have to stay in contact with them if I didn't feel good about it and that I didn't have to let them come to my graduation. It was totally up to me. Bob and Peg would support me, no matter what I decided.

It took me a day or two to get back to normal, but being around the Brandt kids always made things better. Someone was always making me laugh and helping me forget that I had ever been sad.

M

CONFIRMATION, AND BIG DECISIONS

After we had figured out that I had already been baptized, I started RCIA (Rite of Christian Initiation of Adults) classes. If you want to be confirmed in the Catholic church, RCIA classes will guide you through your journey. My classes led up to Easter, and I would be confirmed at an Easter Mass.

Part of the confirmation process involves selecting your godparents. I chose Monica Flakus, my school counselor, to be my godmother. We had bonded, and she had helped me so much when I enrolled at Wahoo Neumann. I then asked Bob Chvatal to be my godfather. Bob and his wife Missy were close friends with the Brandts and were two of the first people I'd met when I moved into the Brandt household. They were always kind to me, and they always helped with the kids when Bob and Peg were gone.

It felt great to be confirmed and to take my first steps into the church as a Catholic. I felt like I was making progress in my faith journey and becoming even more united with the Brandt family.

The other big milestone on the horizon was my high school graduation. School was coming to an end, and I needed to figure out what to do after graduation. I had been thinking about cosmetology school because I had always loved doing hair, but everyone else was planning to enroll in a four-year college program. For example, Tia had decided to go to Benedictine College in Atchison, Kansas, where she would also play basketball.

I decided to discuss my plans with some of my teachers. When I brought up my idea about going to cosmetology school, one teacher said, "Why would you do that when you have worked hard to finish twelve years of school? You should build on what you have done. You should get a college degree that means something." I looked at her in shock and walked away wondering if I should take her advice.

I had no idea how to apply for college, but with help from my family I was able to send out a few applications. I wasn't sure that I would be accepted anywhere because my grades were average and my SAT and ACT scores were not very strong. Nevertheless, we sent in the applications and waited to hear back.

Meanwhile, I decided to make a phone call to my cousin Corey. I was nervous but also excited to reconnect with him.

Corey answered when I called, and he sounded shocked and excited too. I told him that I had reconnected with Earl and Beth and had asked them for his phone number.

We talked for about an hour, and then he invited me to visit him at the house where he lived with his mom and grandmother.

Before we ended the call, I told Corey that I still had the pink cat his mom had given me and that I couldn't wait to tell her I had kept it through all my moves.

I hung up and felt really good about making the phone call. It was great to have at least one good connection from my past.

A few days later I drove to Kate's house with butterflies in my stomach. I wondered what Corey, Kate, and Nan looked like now. I was curious about how they would react and whether they would be excited to see me.

As I pulled into the driveway, Corey immediately came out to greet me. I couldn't get out of my car fast enough! I ran up and gave him a big hug. We hugged for a long time, and I was smiling ear to ear. Then we walked into the house and Kate greeted me right away. She gave me a hug and said that Nan was downstairs. She told us to visit with Nan first and that she would be down a little later. Corey led me downstairs to Nan's apartment, and even though she had aged, she still looked beautiful. I think I had expected her to look the same way she had looked when I was a child.

Nan and I hugged, and then Corey and I talked for hours about our childhood. We laughed as we remembered that all the cousins had played football when we gathered for Thanksgiving and that we had spent most of our time playing together at Kate's house during the summer. I had vivid memories and it felt good to revisit them! As fun as it was to discuss those memories, we didn't talk about what had happened to me or why I had been removed from the family. It was as if the separation had never happened. We didn't discuss what had happened to me afterwards either. We talked about what I wanted to do after I graduated, but that was it when it came to my life.

It was getting late, so we decided to wrap things up and Corey walked with me to my car. Before getting into my car, I asked him if he ever talked to Patrick. He said that they hadn't spoken in a long time. We said our goodbyes, and he promised to stay in touch and to come to my graduation.

As I drove off, I was grateful and happy to have been able to reconnect with Corey. I thought the visit had gone well, but there was something about Kate that just didn't feel right.

It was as if she had been pretending to be excited to see me. I don't know if she was uncomfortable because I was her sister's child and things hadn't worked out or if something else was bothering her. I decided not to think about it too much because maybe she was just nervous.

I reflected on all the things that happened during the previous few weeks. I had reconnected with the Butlers, Corey, Kate, and Nan, all of whom had played key roles in my childhood. It was a lot to process! It felt good in a way, and yet I was disappointed because I hadn't reconnected with Patrick. I told myself that I needed to take things one step at a time.

When I got home, I saw an envelope from Kearney State University addressed to me. I picked it up and took a deep breath as I opened it. I read the letter but couldn't believe what it said: I had been accepted! I ran into the living room to tell the family, but no one was there. I looked outside and saw them sitting by the pool, and then I quickly ran out and told them my news. Everyone was so excited for me!

I couldn't wait to call Kari because I knew she was planning to attend college in Kearney also. She and I were best friends, and I was glad we would have that friendship to rely on as we started our college years. Tia and I talked later that night about how excited we were about going to college. As we talked, it started to hit us that we would soon be apart and moving in separate directions. It started to bring me down a bit because I had come to rely on Tia. We quickly reminded each other that we still had a few weeks of high school left and then the entire summer. We were determined to make the most of our time together!

It had been a full day, and my mind was filled with thoughts as I drifted off to sleep. I had grown to love the day-to-day routine in the Brandt household, but change was inevitable.

P

FIGURING IT OUT ON MY OWN

High school graduation came and went, and now it was time to figure out my next steps. Most of my friends had enrolled in college and were preparing for the next school year. I had not done the same for a few reasons.

First, my parents did not have enough money to cover college. I could have applied for student loans like some of my friends, but I wasn't sure what I wanted to do. I didn't want to take out loans and waste time if I didn't have a focus. I also wanted to move away from home as quickly as possible. I had been waiting for a long time to finally get away from my parents. To do that, I needed to work to support myself. In the end I told myself I wouldn't take any steps toward college until I knew what I wanted to do.

I found a full-time job and then went apartment hunting. I ended up moving into an apartment with a friend, and this started the journey that I would continue on for the next several years. My life between the ages of 18 and 24 can be best summed up by saying that it was "real-world trial and error" every step of the way.

Living in an apartment with a roommate was the first time I had been out on my own. I was working but didn't have much money. My roommate was in his first year of college and didn't have much money either. To cover costs, we got creative and came up with a fun side hustle. Since we were still eighteen, we weren't old enough to buy alcohol, but one of our friends could. Twice a month we paid our friend to pick up a keg of beer for us. We had already sent out word to our friends that we would be hosting a party. Ten dollars at the door got you a Solo cup and all the beer you could drink, provided the keg didn't run out. Of course, our goal was to bring as many people in the door as possible. It worked like a charm, and we drained a keg twice a month.

One of the agreements we made with each other was that the apartment had to be cleaned the day after each party, and we would also split all of the proceeds evenly. Our parties helped to cover part of our rent, utilities, and food, relieving some of our financial pressure. I continued to hold full-time jobs and luckily, they were with companies that were growing. This gave me a chance to gain experience and move up the management ladder.

I managed stores for Blockbuster Video and then managed customer service teams at Best Buy. Each of those jobs gave me a stable income and experience that would become invaluable. I learned how to manage people in busy environments, as well as how to handle situations with customers. I also learned about systems and how to master them. All of that experience paid off later in my career.

I still needed extra money, though, so I picked up a part-time job that still stands out as one of the best jobs I've ever had. I took a part-time position at the Funnybone Comedy

Club working the door, handling the sound system for the stage, and helping to clean and set up the room before and after each show. The club was managed and owned by Colleen Quinn, who would become a friend and mentor. To this day, I haven't met anyone else who is as genuinely cool or inspiring. As a single mother, Colleen was raising two boys while running one of the most successful comedy clubs in the country.

The Funnybone job gave me an opportunity to work with a crazy crew, and we did our jobs while amazing comedians took the stage each night. For me personally, it was an opportunity to learn how comedians prepared and delivered their material over and over. I saw how they worked on their delivery and timing, and just as important, I observed how they worked a crowd. That left an impression on me and would later play a big role in my professional life.

I loved that job so much that it never felt like work to me. It was fast-paced as we set up and got the crowd into their seats. Then the lights would go down and the show kicked in. During the show I would make sure the crowd kept quiet, but more importantly I was soaking in what was happening onstage.

Working at Funnybone had a huge impact on my sense of humor. That may sound like a weird thing to say, but it opened me up, and the laughs I had there were truly a release. The saying "laughter is the best medicine" is true! All of this occurred under the watchful eye of Colleen. I was one of many employees who referred to Colleen as "Aunty Fun Fun" and for good reason. There was no one who had more fun or could make us laugh harder! Over the years she played the role of mother or aunt in many people's lives. For comedians, she was someone who helped them get their career in motion or helped propel them to greater heights. For employees, she was the person who kept us together as we dealt with the craziness of our personal lives. For me, she was the picture of a strong, independent woman who had experienced much in her life and now was parenting her children and sometimes us, too! To this day, Colleen continues to be a trusted friend who will make me smile as soon as I see her enter the room. I worked at Funnybone for many years, and to this day I still drop in sometimes to see a set, but more importantly to see Colleen. She has had a profound impact on my life, and I am forever grateful.

Over this span of time, I thought about Melyssa and my family, but now I was doing so on my own. The thoughts were there, but I was making my way in the world and could deal with them in my own space. That worked for a while, but then things took a turn that I didn't expect. Something happened that rocked my world. Once again, I was faced with a situation I didn't know how to handle.

It began with a phone call from my dad. At first it seemed like a normal conversation where he was just checking in, but as we were finishing the call he asked if I would stop by the house. Later that day, I ended up going over, and that was when they dropped a bombshell on me. This time there wasn't a dramatic buildup before they shared their news. Actually, their tone was very matter of fact as they spoke. They let me know they had visited Melyssa and then proceeded to ask me if I wanted to attend her high school graduation with them.

As their words reached my ears and rattled around in my head, all I could do was stare at them. I didn't react in any way. I simply looked away as I tried to process what they had just said to me. I was stunned and didn't want to show them my reaction. My guard had been up for years, and this was yet another reason why I had pulled away from them emotionally. The words that they said were unbelievable. Emotions flooded my head. I couldn't make sense of the news because it was so shocking at that moment.

Hearing them tell me about their meeting with Melyssa caught me off guard and then started to anger me. I didn't want to react in the moment. I wanted to get away and process the news on my own. I told them I needed to think about it and then got up and left. As I drove away, I still couldn't believe what I had just heard. They had visited Melyssa? They had sat face-to-face and spoken with her? This seemed impossible to comprehend.

My mind was filled with questions. When did this happen? Where did this meeting take place? In my mind Melyssa had to have been on the other side of the country. Certainly she was, because she couldn't have been anywhere close to Omaha. Right?

After pondering those questions, I shifted to the question they had asked me: "Would you like to attend Melyssa's high school graduation?" One question had made it out of my mouth before I left their house: "Where is the graduation being held?" The answer floored me. It was in Wahoo, Nebraska! As I pieced this together, I realized that Wahoo was only 30 miles from Omaha. In this case, the saying "so close and yet so far" should have been flipped around. In my head she had felt far away, yet she had been so close.

P

SHOULD I STAY OR
SHOULD I GO?

I t took me a few days to come to grips with the news that my parents had shared with me. As I continued to cycle through the same questions over and over, I struggled with a slew of emotions. I was angry that they had seen my sister and hadn't invited me to go with them. I was sad that she had been so close and yet I had never known about her whereabouts. I was also excited about the prospect of seeing her again.

Even though I wanted to see Melyssa, another thought entered my mind. How was I supposed to attend her graduation and sit with my parents? I was appalled by the thought that my parents and I would be standing side by side as we congratulated Melyssa on her graduation. How could we stand together with smiles on our faces and look at Melyssa as if everything was okay?

How about this for a greeting: "Hi! Congratulations on your graduation! Oh, and sorry about shipping you off into the foster care system!" The more I thought about it, the more upset I became. I wanted to see her more than anything in the world, and yet I was filled with guilt over what my parents had done. There was no way I was going to stand in front of Melyssa and act as if I was okay with what had happened. I was not going to send that message.

Because of those conflicting thoughts, I made a tough decision. I decided not to go to Melyssa's graduation. My decision went against everything that I wanted to do, but I made up my mind and told my parents. I had also made another tough decision: not to pursue Melyssa beyond that. I wanted her to live her life and put the Butler family behind her. I wanted her to move forward and find happiness.

With that in mind, I decided that I shouldn't interfere because I thought it would be selfish to do so. Melyssa was about to take the next step in her life after graduation, and I wanted her to have the chance to start fresh. If that meant that I needed to stand back instead of trying to jump into her life after ten years of separation, then I had to live with it. I felt like I was choosing the right path since my family had been the ones who had created the situation. I thought that in Melyssa's mind I would always be attached to what they had done and that she wouldn't want the negative association that I might bring.

In the end, my parents ended up attending, and I tried to move on. We didn't talk about it (shocker), and I was living on my own so I could stay as far away from them as I wanted to. In doing so, I worked hard to bury the emotions I was feeling. My guilt and shame were strong, and I wanted to run away and not have it burden her, or me.

Part of dealing with my emotions meant finding new ways to manage them. I discovered that I could "self-medicate" if I wanted to have fun and forget about my troubles. Hey, I was in my early twenties and that meant I could go out and let loose.

During those years I had been involved in a few relationships. One of them was serious, and for two months we ran off to another state to start over. I jumped into that relationship because I wanted to help her overcome some of her personal issues. It wasn't a good decision, so I came back and ended up in another relationship where I could run in a different way. I wanted to escape, and my relationship allowed me to do so by engaging in plenty of drinking and recreational drug use.

On the weekends, we went to bars and made sure we had plenty of extras to keep us going. I'm not going to lie and say that I didn't have fun. Our circle of friends partied a lot, and it also gave me a way to escape from the past.

It may have seemed like I was reliant on chemicals to enjoy life or to run from the past, but I was still in control. I was fortunate to be able to stop whenever I chose to, and that was exactly what I did one morning. I had been living in this cycle for a few years until one morning when things started to feel different.

I was living in an apartment with my girlfriend, and I was getting ready for work. My girlfriend had already left for the day and I had stepped out of the shower. As I looked at my reflection in the bathroom mirror, I saw exhaustion on my face. I was in a routine of bringing myself up and down chemically, and it had started to take a toll. I kept looking at myself, and then I started to question what I was doing and where I was going with my life.

I remembered when I had told myself I would go to college as soon as I knew what I wanted to do. Well, that hadn't happened yet, and I was now 24. I felt physically and mentally drained. I had been pushing away thoughts and feelings that had brought me down. I didn't have to deal with my parents or my memories of the past, and I was choosing my own path.

Now my path had led me to this moment where I was questioning my decisions. I stared at my reflection as thoughts raced through my head, and then something clicked in my mind. I looked away and then turned back toward the mirror.

I knew it was time to stop using alcohol and drugs to chase away my thoughts and feelings. To do that, I would have to change my living situation. The relationship with my girlfriend had become reliant on regular partying. If I was going to change, it would mean changing everything.

I called my workplace and then started packing. Within a few hours I had moved out of the apartment and was ready to start a new chapter.

The conversation with my girlfriend didn't go well, but then again, most breakups don't. My decision had been quick and impulsive, but it was the right thing to do. It was time for me to move forward in a big way.

M

GRADUATION

G raduation day was here, and it felt bittersweet. Graduating from high school was awesome, but the prospect of moving on to college made me feel sad. I felt like I had finally found out where I was supposed to be. On top of that, one part of my life was coming full circle: I would see the Butlers at the graduation ceremony and finally see Patrick again. I could end my high school years by reconnecting with my long-lost brother!

The buildup to the ceremony made it seem like it would be bigger, but in truth, the ceremony only lasted about twenty minutes. I used a portion of that time to carefully scope out the audience. It didn't take me long to find the Butlers. My heart leapt as I scanned their faces. Earl, Beth, and Dere had made it, but Patrick was nowhere to be found. I was sad to realize that he wasn't there, but I wasn't going to let his absence ruin my day. Maybe he had a good reason for not coming. I wanted to give him the benefit of the doubt.

After the graduation ceremony, we gathered in the hallways at school to say goodbye to some of our friends and to take photos. It was wild to be celebrating while realizing that I wouldn't see some of those familiar faces again.

The Brandt family surrounded us as we continued to talk and take even more photos. As we were talking, I turned around and saw that the Butlers were standing off to the side quietly watching us. I immediately walked over and thanked them for coming and mentioned that they could follow us to the house where we were holding our graduation party. Before I left, I asked them where Patrick was. They gave the same response they had given before: "He couldn't make it." I nodded and then turned and rejoined the family. As I walked away, I felt sad because I had felt sure that Patrick was going to be there. Certainly he would have wanted to talk to me.

The house was filled with family and friends ready to celebrate with Tia and me. Prudy had made the trip as well! Bob and Peg made sure that Tia and I were equally recognized, going so far as to have two separate cakes. Conversations were taking place all over the house, and I moved from room to room to thank everyone.

The Butlers showed up, but I didn't get a chance to talk much with them. They sat off by themselves and literally looked like they were attending a funeral. They still didn't know how to react to me or to the Brandt family. I was torn because I wanted to make them feel welcomed, but I didn't have time to figure out how to do that. It was my graduation day, and I wasn't going to let them get me down.

They soon got up, and before they left the house, Earl told me how proud they were of me. Beth stood next to him and thanked me for letting them come. It felt awkward once again.

After the Butlers left, Corey and a few of his friends showed up, which meant the world to me! Corey even brought me a huge brown teddy bear that I still have to this day. He said it was for a fresh start!

The entire day was a mix of emotions. I felt excited to have reached graduation day, but I also felt a mixture of joy and sadness as I bounced between friends, new family members, and "old" family members. Having the Butler family attend had not turned out the way I had expected. Deep down I had hoped that it would allow me to see Patrick. When he didn't show up, I felt great disappointment. His absence left me with more questions than answers. I had hoped that talking with him could help me resolve my feelings about the past and possibly allow us to rebuild our relationship.

It would take a while for me to process all of my emotions and then continue to move forward. Plenty of good memories were made on graduation day, and I recognized that one chapter of my life was ending and a new one was beginning.

M

INTO THE DORM

I was thankful that Kari and I would be going to the same college, but we decided not to room together because we had heard stories about it ruining some friendships. We figured we would be around each other enough anyway.

Because of that decision, I needed to find a roommate. I reached out to a friend I had met when I was in high school in Bellevue. I thought about her one day and took a chance and called her. Her name was Brittany, and we immediately picked up where we had left off. During our conversation, we realized that we were going to attend the same college. We laughed and decided that we should room together. Just like that, I was set to begin school.

Summer was coming to an end, and I was ready to start a new chapter at the University of Nebraska's Kearney campus. I was grateful that the first year would be filled with general studies, because I had no idea what I wanted to do. Tia and I loaded all my belongings into my little red Toyota Tercel and drove off, while Bob and Peg followed us in their car with more of my things.

Driving away from the Brandt house was hard. I felt sad because I wouldn't see the Brandt kids daily anymore. I had started to consider them my siblings and had grown accustomed to being part of a tightly knit family. Bob and Peg were amazing and had done so much for me in a short amount of time. Now here we were with loaded cars, driving me off to college.

Tia and I had made each other a tape of songs that we both loved, and we sang our hearts out all the way to Kearney. It was a great road trip that filled my heart with joy!

After arriving on campus, we found my dorm room and started the process of moving in. Brittany had already been there and had started to decorate. Dorm rooms aren't huge, so it was an easy setup!

I was in a coed dorm building, and each floor was designated for boys or girls only. Our room had a bathroom that we shared with the girls next door. I met the girls from the connecting room, and they were so friendly that I began to feel a bit less nervous.

We finished decorating and it was time for the Brandts to leave. I felt a huge knot in my stomach and then became very sad. I hate goodbyes, and as I gave everyone a hug I tried not to cry. Of course, that didn't work too well, and I ultimately started crying. They calmed me down and reminded me that they would see me soon.

After they left, I sat on my bed and cried. Brittany was still not there, and everyone else was moving into their rooms. In that moment, I had that familiar feeling of starting over, which had never felt good. I eventually pulled myself together and called Kari to see if she had gotten settled. She was with her boyfriend, who also attended Kearney. She told me there was a party that night and invited me to join them if I wanted to. That sounded great! I told myself that I needed to keep busy. Plus, the party would be a way to meet other people. Let's get this new chapter started!

M

FIRST YEAR AND A WARNING

My first year of college was off to a quick start, and I had already met large numbers of people in the dorm, in my classes, and at a variety of parties.

Many of the parties were held at sororities, and many of the girls I met asked me if I was going to "rush." Several of them had already started the process and were now waiting to see which house they would end up in. I loved the idea of being in a sorority because it would mean having instant friends and parties, but the dues were expensive and I didn't know if I could afford them. I hadn't given the idea of joining a sorority much thought beyond that, so I hadn't pursued it.

At that point, it was too late for me to rush. I wasn't aware of it yet, but there was another way to get into a sorority. A girl who was already in a sorority could select me and then help nominate me to join her house. That was exactly what occurred when I heard a knock on my dorm room door one day. When I opened the door, I saw a girl I had met at a few sorority parties. Her name was Kimberly, and she was a member of the Chi Omega sorority. As we greeted each other, I noticed that she was holding a cup filled with candy and it had Greek letters on the outside. She extended the candy-filled cup and explained that she wanted to nominate me to be her "little sister" in Chi Omega.

During our conversations at a few parties, Kimberly and I had discovered a connection: she had grown up about 20 minutes outside of Wahoo, and her grandmother was a neighbor of the Brandts. Now she was asking me to join her in a sorority. I couldn't believe it! She told me to think about it and to let her know by the end of the week. She also told me to call her "Berly" for short. I told her I would have to think it over and see if I could afford the dues.

After Berly left my room, I immediately called the Brandts to share my news. They were happy for me but also told me that if I wanted to join the sorority, I would need to figure out how to pay the dues because they would not cover the cost. Each of the kids in the family had to earn their way through school, and this expense was no different.

I could tell that Bob and Peg didn't think that joining the sorority was a great idea, but I wanted to be like the other girls and fit in. Suddenly, I was picturing myself wearing Greek apparel, going to functions, and having even more fun! As a sorority member, I might be more popular. I thought about it for a day and then decided to let Berly know I was in! I had saved money from working during the summer, and I could use some of it to pay my dues. I also had a work study job that could bring in some additional money.

I was accepted, and I loved being a Chi Omega. We attended meetings on Mondays where we would learn about the history of our sorority. We were also required to maintain a certain number of study hours at the house. Mixed in with all of that were quite a few fundraisers and a bunch of parties.

I wasn't crazy about all the meetings and study hours, but I loved spending time with my sorority sisters.

Keeping up with school and the sorority kept me so busy that I didn't have much time to spend with Kari. She was also busy with school, as well as spending time with her boyfriend. Kari lived in a different dorm, which meant we couldn't just walk down the hall to say hello. We had been best friends in high school and had thought that we would stay tight during our college years as well. I had never expected college to be so busy that we would not have much time together.

My roommate Brittany and I were also drifting in different directions. We didn't see each other all the time, so I tried calling her several times to see if she wanted to hang out, but she always said no. I invited Brittany to participate in some of the things that I was doing, but she didn't seem interested. I noticed that she was sleeping a lot and starting to detach from people in the dorm.

About a month and a half into the school year, I walked into our dorm room and discovered that Brittany had moved out. I immediately called her to find out what was going on. She told me she had dropped out of school because she didn't like it there and was going to take some time to figure things out. Just like that, I had a dorm room to myself. Within the next week that quickly changed, though. I ended up hanging out with some of the girls across the hall and met one of their friends who had a bad roommate situation brewing. As we talked throughout the night, I told her that I had a solution for her. She could move in with me and take Brittany's spot. A few days later she did just that, and during the rest of the school year my dorm life went smoothly.

Finishing the school year academically was a challenge. I had not been a strong student in high school. Now the stakes were higher, and so was the workload. My test grades were up and down, and I had trouble keeping up with schoolwork. I made it to the end of the school year but barely passed. At semester's end, I packed up my things and headed back to Wahoo for the summer. I had missed everyone and was eager to go back.

I had been home for about three weeks when I received a letter from the college informing me that I was going to be placed on academic probation. I needed to write a letter stating why I should be given an opportunity to continue attending school at Keaney.

I was nervous, and I knew that I needed to talk to Bob and Peg and explain my situation. I thought I was going to be in trouble and that they would be disappointed. We sat down that night and discussed it. They listened and then calmly asked me if I wanted to continue with school. I said yes and asked them if we could write a letter together. Weeks later I was relieved to get a response stating that I could continue to attend school. I needed to improve my grades, though, or I would be back to square one. I felt optimistic, but I wanted summer to last as long as possible!

M

WHAT'S YOUR NAME, AND WHERE DO YOU GO TO SCHOOL?

As summer rolled on, I knew one thing for sure: the Brandts were my people, and I couldn't imagine not having them in my life. I decided to do something to make sure that things wouldn't change. I found the courage to ask Bob and Peg if they would adopt me. Their answer was not what I had expected. It wasn't a matter of them not wanting to adopt me; instead, they couldn't do it because I was too old to be eligible for adoption. I was disappointed, but I understood. I then asked them a different question: "What if I changed my name?" I knew in my heart that I did not want to have "Fliehmann" as my last name anymore! I wanted to be a Brandt. Bob smiled and said, "Now, *that* is not a problem!"

On August 3, 1992, I officially became a "Brandt." From that moment forward, I could call them Mom and Dad and know in my heart that it was true. The legal process was interesting. I could change my first, middle, and last name if I wanted. I decided to change the spelling of my first name back to what

I had originally been given. It meant changing the "i" back to "y." I decided to keep my middle name as "Ann." I think if I had the choice today, I would have changed it back to "Dawn," but back then I think I still held so much anger toward the Unrau family that I couldn't imagine having a name that sounded like "Don" (Mr. Unrau's first name). Even though it was a totally different spelling, it reminded me of him. I would now begin my second year of college with a different last name, and I was planning to work hard to get out of academic probation.

My roommate from the end of the freshman year returned, and we picked up right where we had left off… sort of. She stayed in the dorm for three weeks and then announced that she was going to move into a house off campus. Once again, I had a room to myself, and I decided to keep it that way for a while. I knew I had to pick things up academically to raise my grades. I tried to focus more in certain areas, but try as I might, I wasn't doing very well in any of my classes.

As the semester was coming to an end, I realized that the main reason I wasn't doing well was that deep down, I knew this wasn't the educational path I wanted to pursue. I knew in my heart that I wanted to do hair, but I had convinced myself that I needed to go to a four-year college instead of cosmetology school. Looking back, I knew that I should have trusted myself and gone for it. The social part of college was fun, but I needed to go after what I wanted as well. I made up my mind that at the end of the semester I would withdraw from the university.

I felt confident about my decision, and when it came time to tell Bob and Peg, I wasn't nervous. They were very supportive and ended up helping me apply to cosmetology school.

It felt strange to be living at home again. I had found a new sense of freedom in college. I missed partying and coming home whenever I felt like it! To get that freedom back, I would have to get a job where I would earn enough money to rent an apartment. I wasn't going to begin my schooling for a few months, so it was the perfect opportunity to work and save as much money as possible.

I ended up applying to many different businesses, but it was tough to find a good fit.

I was getting frustrated, but finally I ended up getting a call for an interview at Lincoln Catholic Social Services. I was nervous because it was a secretarial position and I didn't have that type of experience. The good news was that it was a temporary position that needed to be filled until the person who held it returned from maternity leave.

Even though I didn't have all the necessary skills, they gave me a shot. It was going to be trial and error with different parts of the job, but they were willing to work with me because they needed to have someone there even if I didn't know how to do everything.

I decided to give it my best effort and work through the next few months until cosmetology school began. It was a learning experience for sure, but somehow I stayed with it until school began. I found out that secretarial work was not right for me, but I was proud of the work I did to support them. I was also thankful that they had taken a chance on me even though I didn't have all the skills they needed. In the end, it was a win for both of us.

M

BACK IN SCHOOL, BACK IN TROUBLE

It wasn't long before I wrapped up the secretarial job and enrolled at the College of Hair Design in Lincoln. I needed to get up early to arrive on time, since it took over 30 minutes to drive from Wahoo. After my morning commutes began, I wanted to move out of the house as soon as possible so I could live in Lincoln and have a shorter drive. That meant saving up money and hopefully finding a roommate to share an apartment.

I fell in love with hair school as soon as I started. It was so much fun to work around people who loved doing hair as much as I did! I began to learn much more about hair and could have great conversations with other students who shared my excitement. It didn't take long to find a group of girls who became friends, and suddenly our days were even more fun as we laughed and shared our stories.

More good news came when I found a roommate. Her name was Cindy, and she was a few months ahead of me in school. Our friendship had grown as we spent time together on the hair-cutting floor or during lunch breaks. We hit it off quickly and decided that both of us could benefit from becoming roommates. She was living in an apartment next door to the school but was looking to live elsewhere just to change things up. We quickly found an apartment that suited us and moved in as soon as we could.

Living in Lincoln meant I didn't have to drive 30 minutes to school and back every day, so I could sleep a little later in the morning. I also found a job at an ice cream parlor, and with my earnings there, plus the tips that I received at hair school, I was able to make ends meet. I was now living my best life! I was out on my own, I had a great group of friends, and I was going to school to prepare me for work that I loved.

As my circle of friends grew, we found ourselves going out regularly at night. I wasn't 21 yet, but on certain nights of the week we could get into a few bars, which was a ton of fun! We made sure we didn't miss those nights! The downtown area of Lincoln was great because there was a block of bars on each side of the road that we could hop between.

We made our way through the bars and had fun talking to new people, dancing, and laughing our way through each night! It wasn't long before that lifestyle caught up with me, though. I started missing school because I was tired from going out the night before. Lack of sleep made it harder to pay attention during classroom lectures.

I started skipping classes and getting into arguments with Mrs. Howard, who owned the college. She was always correcting me or making a comment about something I was doing. I felt like I was continually being singled out when she said these things. The comments made me dread interacting with her, and one day, one of her random remarks pushed me too far. She asked me why I hadn't cleaned up a pile of hair color bowls when they were nowhere near the station that I was working at. She made the comment in front of a few other students, and it embarrassed me. I reacted in anger, calling her a "bitch" in front of the group that was standing near us. Everyone who heard me was shocked, and I was promptly asked to leave the class that day.

Unfortunately, a few similar interactions would happen in the following weeks with other instructors. I was reacting in anger each time something was said to me that I didn't like. I had built up a story that they were against me and my outbursts were my way of defending myself. I was sent home each time I reacted angrily. I would shrug it off, head home and go to sleep, and then get up and get ready for my night job or go out with my friends.

After each of these blow-ups, I would return to school the next day thinking that I'd be in trouble, but nothing would happen. I carried on without thinking too much of it and ignored Mr. and Mrs. Howard. (Mr. Howard was the son of Mrs. Howard.) One day I went off on one of the instructors who had been asking me all kinds of questions. It felt like she was being annoying on purpose, and I said, "Why are you being a bitch and asking me all these questions? There are other people in the class! Talk to them!" Once again, I had reacted angrily because I thought I was being singled out. Of course, I was asked to leave the class immediately and go to the office. Instead, I went home and took a nap before going out with my friends later that night.

This pattern of getting into trouble and going home brought consequences that I had not expected. Going home meant missing out on hours that I needed to graduate, so it was now going to take longer for me to finish school. My attitude was not great, but I didn't care as much as I should have cared at the time. I preferred going out with my friends because it was more fun than being in school.

One day I went back to school but was told that I couldn't go to class until I met with Mr. Howard. I was immediately annoyed, but I went into his office. He started by saying, "You can't just leave school when you get into trouble. You need to come to the office when you are told. You also need to be respectful to the instructors and to Mrs. Howard. This isn't the first time you have been disrespectful, and you need to apologize."

I got angry and yelled out, "I'm not apologizing to that bitch!" As soon as I said it, I noticed that someone was standing in the doorway of the office. I was stunned to look over and see my dad. I couldn't believe it. Mr. Howard had called him to tell him why we were having a meeting. I just stared straight in front of me and didn't make eye contact with either of them.

My dad told Mr. Howard we were going to leave for a bit and then come back.

Mr. Howard said, "In order to come back, she needs to apologize to Mrs. Howard and to Rose, the instructor."

As we walked out the door, I was thinking, "Like hell will I apologize. I have nothing to apologize for." In the Brandt family, it was a common occurrence to go on a "car ride" with Dad if you were in trouble. Sometimes it was just a talk, and at other times you might get lectured quite sternly! You literally had to listen because you were in a car with nowhere else to go. The rides were meant to let us blow off steam, but also for Dad to help us understand what was wrong with our actions and figure out how we were going to fix a situation. As you can imagine, when we left the cosmetology school that day, I was in for a long car ride! Dad told me, "You can't just lose it and call whoever you're mad at a name and then expect to not be in trouble."

I knew that to finish school I would have to apologize, but I just looked straight ahead and said, "I don't have anything to apologize for. They need to just mind their own business and leave me alone."

"That's not how it works," Dad said. "We will have a meeting this afternoon, and you must go back and apologize. This isn't an option; this is your future, and you need to do this if you want to finish school. You are in the wrong, and now we need to fix it. Not apologizing is not an option."

I looked out the window and said, "I just can't apologize." My defenses were up, and I didn't feel that I should apologize. Part of it was a defense against feeling rejected. If I was being singled out, it felt like I was doing something wrong and would be rejected for it. I felt like I had been rejected by so many different people throughout my life, and this situation seemed to build on that feeling. Because of that, I was keeping my guard up, which made it difficult for my dad to deal with.

We ended up going back that afternoon and heading to Mr. Howard's office. Dad did most of the talking and basically apologized for me and told them that I would do better. I was given another chance, and it was only because Dad had fought for me.

I was surprised at how it all went down and that Dad had stood by my side and fought for me. No one had ever done that before, and this was another sign that the Brandts loved me for who I was. I realized that I needed to get my act together and start taking school seriously.

M

WAS THAT WHO I THINK IT WAS?

Cindy and I were still roommates when she passed her cosmetology board exam and began working in a salon. I had two more months left before I graduated, and seeing how well Cindy was doing gave me extra motivation to get the hours and credits I needed.

During my time in school there were always hair shows or classes outside of school that we could attend. We learned about new techniques and products, and we gained different perspectives about the hair industry. These classes could also give us extra credits, which motivated us to attend. They were usually fun, so we liked to go to as many as we could. My friends found a show that was coming up soon, so we decided to make a night of it. We signed up, and when the day came, we met for dinner and then went to the show. We learned a lot during the show, and after it had ended, we decided to tell the educator how much we had enjoyed it.

As we walked through the crowd, I casually glanced at some of the people who were still in the auditorium. Some were talking, and others were heading toward the exit. Do you know how you can walk through a crowd of faces that you don't recognize, and you tune them out as you continue to move? That is what was happening at that moment. I was cruising along with my friends until a face registered with me. I stopped because I couldn't believe it. I was staring at Patrick. He was helping to clear the show stage.

It was a surreal moment. I stood there thinking, "There is my brother. After all this time, there he is." My heart was pounding as I looked around and saw someone from the show and immediately went up to her and asked, "Who is that guy?" She turned and said, "His name is Patrick." It was him. I had known it was, but I wanted to hear it. He hadn't seen me yet, so I made my way over. As I approached, he was still focused on cleaning things up. I broke the silence quickly.

"Patrick? It's me, Melyssa."

He stopped and turned toward me. The look on his face was one of pure shock. It was like he had seen a ghost. A few seconds passed, and then he asked, "What... what are you doing here?" He looked even more stunned when I explained that I was in hair school in Lincoln and my friends and I had come to the show for extra credit.

It was my turn to be surprised when he said, "I am going to hair school too! In Omaha. I'm getting credit for helping with this show." We let the fact that we were both attending cosmetology school at the same time sink in. That was a crazy coincidence in and of itself! Our brief interaction was quickly broken up, though. The people who were cleaning up after the show continued to work around us and were trying to finish, and at the same time my friends had closed in and wanted to head out for the night. We were both feeling the pressure to wrap things up.

"It was great to see you. I'm sorry that I need to finish up," Patrick said.

I smiled and replied, "Yes, for sure! Great seeing you, too!"

And with that, I turned and headed out with my friends. I was excited beyond belief, but I was also confused. I couldn't believe what had just happened! His reaction was not what I had envisioned when I dreamt of us meeting again, though. He didn't seem as excited to see me as I was to see him. Was it just that he was surprised? I replayed the scene over and over in my head as we left.

The group ended up going out that night, and along the way I met up with Cindy. I immediately told her what had happened. In my group of friends, she was the only one who knew my story. She was excited for me, but as we continued to talk, I realized that Patrick and I had not asked for each other's phone numbers. She wanted to know if I was going to try to get his contact information, and I told her that I didn't think so.

"He literally looked like he had seen a ghost and couldn't get out of there fast enough. He probably had forgotten about me, and we literally have nothing in common, so I'm not going to pursue it."

I wanted to change the subject, so we joined the rest of the group and continued with our night.

Over the next few weeks, I couldn't get Patrick out of my mind. I wished that we would have had more time to talk. I'm sure if we did, he would have gotten over the initial shock of seeing me and it would have gone well.

I couldn't believe that we were both in hair school! What else had happened in his life? I had so many questions. My thoughts would then shift, and I would get so angry about how I had been robbed of a relationship with my brother. I literally had nothing to show for my past and didn't have a relationship with him. It was frustrating, and I continued to wrestle with these thoughts as time went by.

A few months later, I graduated from cosmetology school and began preparing for the board exams. I was incredibly nervous. I usually didn't do well on tests, but I knew I had to pass this one to be able to pursue my career.

The exams consisted of a written test and a practical exam. I prepared as well as I could, and then my day finally came. The exams went more quickly than I expected, and then I had to wait until the results were mailed to me. I finally received the letter two weeks later. I had passed the practical exam! I was so excited!

My eyes scanned the next page, and as I read the results of my written test, my heart sank. I had failed the written test by 2 points! I was devastated! The good news was that I had an opportunity to retake the test, and the bad news was that I would have to wait three months to do so. I planned to study during the next three months to make sure I passed. While that was going on, I planned to go back to school!

I was close to receiving my cosmetology license, and I decided to build on that and enroll in the barbering program. Just when I had thought I was done with school, I was heading back for more! Having a dual license would help me in my career, so I figured that this was the time to do it. I had found my groove in school after my bumpy start and had gotten along well with the instructors and the owners. I was able to start the barbering program immediately, and it helped to pass the time before I could retake my cosmetology exam. The first three months were great, and the extra hair cutting techniques helped me improve.

Finally it was time for me to take the written exam again, and I went into it feeling confident. I finished quickly, and then the waiting game began. The two weeks once again dragged by slowly until the mail finally arrived with the letter from the state. I opened it quickly and couldn't believe my eyes. I had

PASSED! I screamed with excitement, called my parents first, and then called all my girlfriends to share the good news! That night the girls took me out and we celebrated!

I had done it! I could finally find a real job where I could earn more money and live my life the way that I wanted! I was ecstatic! Receiving my cosmetology license was a boost, and it suddenly made me question whether I wanted to continue going to school. I now had an opportunity to go right into a salon and start earning money, and that proved to be a strong draw for me. I decided to make the move and leave the barbering program. I felt good about my decision, and my mind was made up. It was time to move forward!

P

HAIR TODAY, BUT
DEFINITELY NOT GONE
TOMORROW

After moving out and getting set up again, I took a few months to work and make a plan. I met up with my friend, Shelly, who was several years into her career. We sat down to talk, and I mentioned that I was ready to go to school. I figured I could start taking classes and declare a major later. She listened and then proceeded to ask me a few questions. She asked me if I wanted to work in a creative field, and I said yes. I enjoyed being creative but didn't know how to channel that energy. She asked if I wanted to be able to build my career at my own pace. I said yes again. She asked if I wanted to work directly with people, and again I replied with a yes. Her next question was one that I had never been asked before: "Would you ever consider doing hair for a living?"

Remember when I said that Shelly was several years into her career? Well, guess what she did for a living? She was a successful hair stylist. Her question caught me off guard. I had never thought about hair styling as a potential career. I then said that it wouldn't hurt to check it out, and with that we set up an appointment to visit the school Shelly had attended. It was the best in the city and had a strong reputation. The more people that I talked to about it, the more I realized how good the school was. I will never know what truly happened the day she took me to visit the cosmetology school. I am still amazed by the fact that I went from taking a simple tour of the school to signing enrollment papers.

I had walked in feeling somewhat unsure, but as I toured the school, I slowly started to picture myself there. I suddenly found myself in a room discussing options, and then a pen was in my hand and I was signing documents. One month later I was sitting in a freshman class. On the first day, we sat in a classroom and the instructor began with simple introductions. She then asked us to share what inspired us to pursue cosmetology as a career. I started to sweat as I listened to all the girls share stories about how they loved doing hair for their friends and families, or how they always played with the hair on their dolls. When my turn came up, all I could squeak out was that my girlfriend had told me that doing hair might be a good career choice for me. I sank into my chair as the girls in the class rolled their eyes.

After that embarrassing moment, my hair education began. I initially thought I would be at a disadvantage in comparison with the other students who had talked about doing hair as they grew up. That thought was washed away when a great instructor said, "They may have played with hair longer than you, but that doesn't mean they have been doing it correctly. You don't have any bad habits to break, but they do." Those words gave me a boost, and after that I dove in. I was 24 and many of the students around me had enrolled after completing high school. They were 18 or 19 and still trying to figure out how to begin life after high school. Since I had shaken things out for several years, I was now facing school as an opportunity to get serious about a career.

I wanted to learn everything that I could, and I went after it with as much energy as I could bring. The owner of the school was an amazing hairdresser who not only owned the school but also ran traveling teams that competed and taught at major shows around the country. He showed me that it was possible to live in Omaha, Nebraska and travel and teach around the world. That opened my eyes to possibilities I hadn't thought of. He taught me not to limit myself and instead to aim far higher than most would.

The advice and inspiration I received from the owner of the school served me well as I began my career. For example, he encouraged me to participate in hair shows and educational demonstrations. Large and small shows are held across the country to educate stylists and barbers about the latest trends, techniques, and products. These shows are held in convention centers, hotel ballrooms, or any space where people can gather.

Because I was close to finishing my schooling, I was asked to help support a small event that was going to be held in Lincoln, Nebraska. It was an easy drive for me, and I was able to help behind the scenes, which gave me an opportunity to learn even more. The demonstration was held in the evening, and just prior to the start I was busy helping the guest artists prepare for the show. I watched as they went on a small stage and started to work on their models. They had a good crowd of maybe 75 people who had bought tickets and wanted to learn more about hair color. The event lasted two hours, and as the show ended, I began to help the artists clean up so we could head back to Omaha.

Many people in the crowd milled about and talked with each other before leaving the venue. As I was picking things up on the stage, I heard someone say my name. I turned around and couldn't believe what I was seeing. Melyssa was standing in front of me. I was so stunned that I couldn't quite process everything that was happening. She quickly said my name and then said, "It's me, Melyssa." I mentioned that I had been assisting at shows because I was in hair school, and then I asked her why she was there. I quickly received another shock as she told me that she was also a cosmetologist and did hair in Lincoln!

So, if you are keeping score at home, that means that not only had Melyssa attended high school 30 miles from Omaha, but she had now moved to Lincoln, which was 50 miles away. She told me that she was attending a cosmetology school in Lincoln. What are the odds that she and her friends would have come to the show that night to attend this class? It was the only class in Lincoln that I had signed up to assist with. Unbelievable.

Melyssa smiled as she told me this, and I just looked at her in disbelief. I had not seen her in person for fourteen years. After making the decision not to attend her high school graduation with my parents, I had chosen not to try and reach out because I thought I should give her space to live her own life. I had buried the feelings I had about doing that and had moved forward. I'd hoped that she had moved forward as well. Now, here she was on a random evening in Lincoln after a hair class, standing face to face with me. We didn't have a lot of time to talk because people were moving around and her friends were ready to leave.

Instead of talking, I'm afraid my body language and facial expression probably said more. I couldn't believe what was happening! And yet there she was. Instantly, I was flooded with feelings of guilt and shame. Leftover shame from the past.

I honestly didn't know what to do. I was completely stunned and couldn't process what was happening.

Melyssa looked happy. She was smiling and engaging as she tried to have a normal conversation with me, but I couldn't get my head around what was happening. She told me that it was good to see me and wished me luck as I finished school. And with that, she and her friends left.

We finished cleaning up the ballroom, and I had a quiet drive home. As I drove, I felt a wave of disappointment wash over me. Why hadn't I said more? Why hadn't I asked Melyssa if we could talk later? Why did I continue to feel wracked with guilt for the past? My feelings of guilt and shame had led me to convince myself that I should leave her alone so that she could live her life without any of that affecting her. Why had I let those feelings continue to influence how I reacted in the moment?

As I drove, I continued to beat myself up with questions and doubts. I would struggle with the same questions for a long time. I had kept my feelings bottled up for years without an outlet, and when I was faced with an opportunity to reconnect, I hadn't known how to react and I shut down.

Around the same time, my parents informed me of a big decision they had made. They let me know that they had decided to end their marriage and were seeking a divorce. Two thoughts entered my mind as I let that soak in. On one hand, I was surprised. Why now? They had gone through so much together and had not ended their marriage when it was really bad. Why end it at this point? On the other hand, it made sense. In fact, I thought they should have divorced many years earlier. Deep down I believed they should have divorced when I was in grade school and that if they had done so, it might have allowed Melyssa to stay in our family.

After hearing the news of their upcoming divorce, I shrugged and said, "So be it." They ended up selling our childhood home and moving into separate homes. Dere stayed with Mom, and Dad lived alone. From that point on, it felt like the distance between all of us increased even more. It was striking to realize that the family had finally broken apart completely. We were all in different places and living our own lives. The "family unit" had shattered, and we would interact on a one-on-one basis only when necessary.

If anything, my parents' divorce solidified my conviction that I needed to keep pushing to establish myself. I was determined to continue forging my own path.

M

SETTLING IN, AND OFF TO WORK

Cindy and I had been roommates for a while when she told me she would have to move out. She had found out she was pregnant, and she needed to move back home to save money. I was sad because she had been such a great roommate and friend.

I now had to decide whether to live alone or to find another roommate. I decided to live by myself, but that ended when I realized it was much cheaper to have a roommate! Luckily, my friend Kristy from hair school was trying to get out of a bad roommate situation, and we decided moving in together would solve both of our problems. It was a win-win for both of us because I could pay my bills and not feel like I was drowning, and she was in a better living environment!

I had also started looking for a job and had been applying at various salons in Lincoln. One of them was called Great Expectations, and they were hiring immediately. I could start that week. The salon was part of a chain and was busy, which could help me immediately. It was fun right from the start, and I quickly fit in with the other stylists. The salon had great energy and I was busy right away.

Not long after I started working at Great Expectations, Kristy graduated from hair school and decided to apply there as well. We were busy enough that she was able to get hired and joined us immediately. Things were going great for the two of us! Our apartment situation had worked out, we both were working in the salon, and we could go out with friends whenever we wanted!

I finally felt stable, and my life was going great. It was also a bonus to be within 30 minutes of my family. I felt at peace knowing I had a family to go home to whenever I wanted. My life was busy, but I enjoyed balancing all of it. Socializing was still a big thing for me and my girlfriends. We would typically go out to the bars on Thursday, Friday, and Saturday nights, and even though it was fun to be with my girlfriends, I was starting to think about dating someone. I had dated a few guys here and there, but nothing had ever developed. I started to wonder if I would ever meet someone who would really click with me.

M

MEETING ALBERT

As I went out with my friends, I kept spotting one particular guy in some of the bars we went to. We never spoke, but he had an amazing smile that caught my attention and stayed with me. I asked my friends if they knew him, and one of them said that she did. She said his name was Albert and she thought he was a nice guy.

Sure enough, my friends and I were out one Saturday night and I happened to spot Albert once again. I was dancing with my friends in a group, and he came up and joined us. Before I knew it, he and I were dancing! After we left the dance floor, we chatted a bit and then went our separate ways.

As the night came to an end, I started looking for him. That didn't work so I asked one of his friends if he had seen Albert, and he said that Albert had left. I asked him if he had Albert's phone number, and he wrote it down for me. I couldn't wait to call him!

When I got home I called him, but a girl answered his phone! I was shocked but then thought maybe he had a female roommate. I asked if he was there, and she said no but that she would have him call me if I left my number. I gave her my number and then hung up. I had no faith that he would call me because I seriously doubted that the girl would forward my message to him.

Well, I was completely wrong. Albert did call, and he said that his best friend Linda was at his house and had given him the message that I had left.

We talked for a bit and then made plans to meet up the next day.

After Albert picked me up, we went to a park where we would have a chance to talk a lot. As we walked, we gradually felt more at ease. The conversation flowed easily, and we both talked about our lives, which helped me understand a lot about him. We talked during the rest of the afternoon, and he cooked dinner for me that evening.

I learned that Albert was from Clemson, South Carolina originally and had come to Lincoln to be on the track team at the University of Nebraska. By the time I met him he had graduated and was a Lincoln police officer. I shared some of my story but mainly talked about things in my life that were more current.

After that night, we started seeing each other often, and eventually I asked him if he wanted to meet my family. I told him my family was big (that was an understatement!), and I reassured him that he would fit right in. He agreed to meet them, and sure enough Albert was an instant hit with everyone!

The night he met my family, we realized that my younger brother Tony had met Albert in the weight room at the University of Nebraska when he had been at a football camp a few years earlier! Small world!

As Albert and I continued to see each other, everything felt like it was starting to fall into place for me. I had a great job where I was building my clientele, I had a great roommate, and now I had a boyfriend. What more could I want? Finally, things were going smoothly for me!

M
REALITY CHECK

I t wasn't long before it felt like the rug had been pulled out from under me once again.

One night Albert and I got together for dinner, but our conversation during the meal wasn't what I had expected. He said he wanted to talk about the future. Unfortunately, the "future" that he referred to involved leaving Lincoln and heading back to the South. He said he didn't like the cold winters in Nebraska and he was ready to leave. I couldn't believe what I was hearing. I was devastated. What was happening?

After Albert went home, I had trouble sleeping as I tried to process what was happening. Things had been going so well, and it had seemed like our relationship was growing. I felt like I didn't have much of a choice about Albert's departure, so I waited to see what would happen next.

During the next week we spent time together every day. As he packed his things and prepared to leave, I watched in disbelief. It was really happening. My heart was breaking, and all I wanted was for him to stay. But he had made up his mind to leave, and I didn't feel like I was reason enough for him to stay.

I kept thinking, "Here we go again." When would someone think I was important enough to make me a priority?

The week ended, and we finally said our goodbyes. I watched as Albert drove off, and then I had to pull myself together and go to work. At the end of my workday, I went home and sat on my bed and cried. My roommate tried to console me and to persuade me to go out, but I was so depressed that I didn't want to do anything. It felt like such a loss.

Each day after that I would rush home and wait for Albert to call me. I would get so excited if the phone rang! On the flip side of that, if he didn't call, it would crush me.

As the weeks went by my routine started to feel somewhat normal again. I slowly started doing things with my friends again just to stay busy and to get out.

I decided that if Albert and I kept in good contact and if things felt right within a year's time, then I would consider moving to where he was… but only if he asked me to join him! To his credit, he kept my spirits up by writing letters, talking with me on the phone, and sending me flowers.

During this time, Albert had settled into his new role as a private investigator who dealt with insurance fraud. He was living in Atlanta and had moved in with a guy who worked with him. Because of that, he now had a permanent spot where I could send letters to him.

When the holidays arrived, we decided it would be fun if I visited him for New Year's Eve. I was so excited to see him! It was my first airplane trip, but the excitement helped me to overcome my nerves.

We had a great weekend! We went to Savannah, Georgia, which had the first beach I'd ever been to. I couldn't believe that I was standing on a beach with my boyfriend as we looked at the ocean!

We also went to Clemson, South Carolina, where I met his family. Albert had an older brother, James, and three younger siblings, Chris, Tyrone, and Tyronza. They were all very kind to me, and it felt great to meet his family. Albert showed me where he had grown up, and then we drove into the mountains and found a waterfall where we sat and talked. It was so beautiful. The next day was New Year's Eve, and we left for Atlanta, where I went to my first concert to ring in the new year. We saw Gerald LeVert and Sinbad and had so much fun laughing and dancing!

The trip had been a whirlwind of fun but was reaching its end. I didn't want it to be over, and I really didn't want to leave.

On our last night together, we made dinner at his place and watched a movie. At different times during the night, I found my emotions getting to me, and I would start to cry. Albert did his best to console me, but my feelings were getting to me. I literally hate goodbyes. To this day, I still don't like them. I think saying goodbye triggers something in me from my past. I would get close to different people in my life, only to be forced to leave them. The goodbyes that had occurred in my past had led to me never seeing some of those people again.

Sometimes I would ask myself if I would ever see Albert again. I had lost Patrick without even having a chance to say goodbye. I had lost other people who were around me. I didn't want to lose Albert.

The next day we did say goodbye, and as I got on the airplane, I couldn't help crying. The passenger next to me was probably wondering who was sitting next to him and what the heck was wrong with me. After I stopped crying, I got lost in my thoughts about my trip.

M

MOVING

During the week after I returned to Lincoln I was in a daze. I felt sad and wanted to be left alone. It took me about a week to get back to normal. As the weeks turned into months, Albert and I kept our communication up, but I started to wonder where things were headed.

Albert ended up getting transferred to Charlotte, North Carolina for his job, and he settled into an apartment. Charlotte was closer to his family, and he was excited to move.

After he got settled, we found ourselves in a similar routine of long-distance calls until he decided enough was enough. He asked me if I wanted to move to Charlotte.

I didn't hesitate to respond with a quick "Yes!" followed by "When?" After the call I was excited to tell my family. My parents had always been so supportive that I felt like the conversation would go well.

Sure enough, after hearing me out they told me that if moving to Charlotte, North Carolina was what I wanted to do, then I should do it. They asked where I was going to live, and I didn't have an answer for them. Well, I did have an answer, but I didn't think I could tell them at the time. I knew I was going to live with Albert, but I also knew that they wouldn't like the idea of us living together without being married. I just told them that I hadn't figured out my living situation yet.

Albert helped me by finding a hair salon that was close to the apartment. He also researched the details about what I had to do to transfer my cosmetology license from Nebraska to North Carolina. Each state has different regulations, and I had to make sure the requirements were met. I ended up only having to pay a fee because I had more hours from my school than North Carolina required, which meant I didn't have to take a state test. One less hurdle to deal with!

Next up was dealing with things back in Lincoln. I told Kristy that I was planning to move out, and I also gave my salon a month's notice. Everyone was happy for me, which was a huge relief. Things were starting to fall into place.

After making my decision, I couldn't wait to leave Nebraska. I was eager to live in a big city and to finally be with Albert. I was going to miss my friends and family, but at 23 that was not enough to keep me from trying something new and being with the man I loved.

With all the excitement, time seemed to fly by. It was almost time for me to leave Nebraska, but I still had one important thing left to do. It was time for me to tell my parents that I would be moving in with Albert. I had considered not telling them and just getting a double landline with a different phone number. Albert didn't think that was a good idea, though. I agreed with him, but I also knew my decision would disappoint them. I knew that it would be better to tell them the truth, and when I did tell them it went better than I'd expected. I knew it wasn't something they approved of, but I just couldn't lie. As we talked, it just reinforced how much they cared about me. My friends at work had a going-away party for me, and we went out one last time to the clubs the night before Albert would fly in.

Albert arrived the next day, and we spent the afternoon packing my things into a U-Haul. After we finished packing, we headed to my parents' house to say goodbye to my family. That was harder than I'd expected. As we were saying goodbye to everyone, my mom took Albert aside to talk to him. I kept my eye on them and wondered what she was saying, but I continued to say my goodbyes to my siblings. After a ton of hugs and tears, we were on our way.

As we drove off, I asked Albert why my mom had taken him aside. He said, "She told me that I had better take good care of you and that I need to make sure that nothing happens to you." I think that made him super nervous, but at the same time he knew that was exactly what he would do. We ended up driving for 22 hours with a few breaks to stretch and eat. I dozed off here and there, but Albert drove us the whole way.

When we arrived in Charlotte, I immediately felt one key difference. The humidity was fierce, and it seemed much hotter than Nebraska. We unpacked the U-Haul and then relaxed the rest of the night. We would have plenty of time to put everything in place later. I was definitely in my happy place!

M
STARTING FRESH

I started my job at The Hair Cuttery, which was located in a great part of Charlotte. It was a very busy shop, and I was able to start building a solid client base quickly. I loved my co-workers and felt like we clicked immediately.

Albert continued to work as a private investigator and then decided to apply for a position at a police department in Charlotte or Gastonia. He would take whichever offer came first. It was a long process, but he ended up getting in with the Gastonia police department. He started on patrol duty and had crazy hours. Each of the officers had to work a shift that would cover a certain part of the day. Some of the shifts were in the morning, while others were overnight. He would work third shift overnight one week, have a few days off, then work second shift during the day, followed by a few days off, and then the next week he would be on first shift in the morning with a few days off. His schedule was not ideal because it didn't allow us to spend much time together.

Our schedules continued to be erratic over the next year. I would occasionally go out with work friends and then Albert and I would try to find time to do something. I started missing my family and friends back home, but I always felt better if

I could talk with them. I started to wonder how things would change so we could gain some consistency.

My answer came on a Friday when Albert and I had some time together. Out of nowhere, he got down on one knee and asked me the big question: "Will you marry me?"

I was shocked but immediately said, "Yes!"

I couldn't wait to call my parents to share the news! That night, Albert and I went to one of his brother's high school football games, and that's where we told his parents. Albert would be the first of his siblings to get married, and his family was thrilled!

On my side of our family, our news added to a busy schedule that was in place. My parents now had three weddings to prepare for within less than two years! My sister Tia's wedding was coming up in September, my sister Tasha's wedding was in August of the following year, and mine would take place the following June.

After setting a date and beginning to plan, I knew one thing for sure: I wanted to be married in Nebraska.

M
WEDDING PLANS

I wanted to keep things simple, but planning a wedding from a distance can be tricky. My mom and sisters stepped up to help with most of the preparations, which was a relief! Since they had things in hand, I could focus on choosing the wedding party.

I knew I wanted my best friend Cindy to be my maid of honor and Tia, Tasha, and Tyronza to be my bridesmaids. Albert's best man was Dan Shonka, who had been his high school track coach, and his brothers would be his groomsmen.

The more I thought about the actual ceremony, the more one thought stayed in my head.

When the bride-to-be walks down the aisle, she typically walks with her father, who then "gives her away" to the groom. I could envision that happening, but I also wanted to make one small change to the routine. My entire life up until that point had been filled with constant change, going from family to family to family. When I ended up meeting the Brandt family, it was the first time in my life that things started to settle down. I wanted Bob to walk me down the aisle as my dad, but I wanted one more person to walk with me as well.

I wanted one person to "give me away" one more time. She was the one person who had been with me from family to family and had performed the unfortunate role of "giving me away" to each family that I ended up with. My original case-worker, Prudy, was the only person in my life who had known me from very early in my life and had stayed with me, even if it was just because she was assigned to me. Each time she'd had to take me to a different family it had felt negative, and now I wanted this moment to turn that feeling around so that her passing me off would be positive.

For the longest time I hadn't liked Prudy because I associated her appearance at my door with having to move away again. It wasn't until I understood what her role was and how much she really cared about my well-being that I started viewing her differently. Prudy had found the Brandts, and if she hadn't matched us up, I don't know where I would have ended up.

I couldn't wait to make the call to ask her if she would walk me down the aisle. When I did, she didn't hesitate to say, "I would be honored!" My heart leapt when I heard those words!

After Prudy said yes, word got out about the wedding and how my caseworker was going to walk me down the aisle. I ended up getting a phone call from the *Lincoln Journal Star* newspaper. They wanted to write a story about our wedding. Their request surprised me, but I said yes because I thought it would be a neat way to share our story. They wanted several details about my life, including how all the moves had brought me to this moment.

Being interviewed for the newspaper article definitely brought up memories from the past that were hard to talk about. I think one of the hardest things was that I hadn't found my brother Patrick. That was difficult to think about because I would have wanted him to be at my wedding.

The article was published, and a few days later I received a phone call from *Woman's Day* magazine. They wanted to do a story about our wedding, too! They called it a fairytale ending and felt that it would fit in well with their magazine. I was excited as I told Albert about the potential article, but he wasn't as excited as I was. He didn't think the whole world needed to know about my life and felt the newspaper article was enough. When we talked, I understood that he wanted to keep things more private. I wanted us to make the decision together, and ultimately we decided not to have *Woman's Day* do the story.

Looking back now, I wish I had made the decision to let them do the story. They were right when they said it was a fairytale ending. I would often tease Albert and say I had missed my chance to meet Oprah. In my mind, my life felt like a story that might have been on Oprah's show!

M

THE BIG DAY

Our wedding day had finally arrived, and things felt like they were happening quickly! I think every bride might say the same thing about her wedding day. Everything was a blur!

Several important moments stood out, however. Albert's family had driven from Clemson, South Carolina, to Wahoo, Nebraska, to be at the wedding. It would be the first time his family had met mine, and I was eager for that to happen!

All of the other familiar wedding details had fallen into place, too. The church looked beautiful, our families and friends surrounded us, and it was time for me to walk down the aisle with Prudy by my side. The traditional walk down the aisle usually consists of the bride's father walking her down to be handed off to the groom. The symbolism is apparent. The father who has watched over the daughter is now allowing the groom to fill that role. In this case, I wanted it to be split. My father, Bob, was going to hand me off, but he had not been in that role while I was growing up. One person had been with me the entire time, though. Prudy had been a part of my life from the beginning. It may not have been easy for her to watch as family after family had passed me off, but throughout the journey, she had kept trying to find the best opportunity for me.

If Prudy had not asked Bob Brandt to meet me while I was in the hospital, I don't know where I would have ended up. My future had changed drastically for the better because of her efforts. I knew I wanted Prudy to walk me halfway down the aisle, and then have my dad walk me the rest of the way. It meant everything to me. At that moment I was filled with nerves, and it seemed to go so quickly.

Looking back now, I am so proud of that moment. It was the perfect way to begin this new chapter of my life. As I took Albert's hand and we stepped forward together, my emotions calmed down. The ceremony was wonderful, and it was a huge thrill to know that we were surrounded by our family and friends.

The reception was pure fun! Everyone was up and dancing, and it was amazing to see both families celebrating with us. Afterwards we made our way to Cancun for our honeymoon, where we relaxed and let things go. It was an amazing start to our married life!

M

THINGS ARE FINE, RIGHT?

When we came back from our honeymoon, we started making decisions about our new house that was being built. It didn't take long before we were getting settled into our new home and making friends with our neighbors. Meanwhile, both of our careers had been progressing. Albert had become a Juvenile Detective, while I had become a manager at The Hair Cuttery.

By this time, Albert had shifted to a consistent schedule with hours that matched mine, which meant that we were able to spend more time together.

As we continued to settle into a routine, it started to feel like "life" was the same, day in and day out. It may sound strange, but I was beginning to question how happy I was. Something felt off, even though things were in a solid place. We had been married for three years, and I had never had someone love me for that long. We had been together for six years if I included the time we had dated. I was also starting to miss my friends back home. I didn't have any close friends in Charlotte, and this was a time in my life when I definitely wanted those types of relationships.

In my head I was starting to build a story that things weren't going as well as I had expected. It was self-sabotage, and I was using it as a defense mechanism in case things didn't work out. In reality, our marriage was going well. I didn't realize that I was carrying a thought in my head—more of a worry that as good as things felt, somehow this would fall apart the way things had done in the past.

I couldn't believe that Albert still loved me as much as he did. How could that be true? I started to tell myself that he would get tired of me and his love would fade, which would mean that he would soon want to leave me. It probably sounds crazy, but I didn't believe he would continue to want to be a part of my life. I started to think I should beat him to it by preparing to end things.

I finally found the courage to talk about my feelings with Albert. We talked a lot, actually! Albert wanted to understand what I was going through and to show me that what I feared wasn't true. Our talks calmed my worries and reassured me that I was with someone who truly loved me.

I regret that I hurt Albert because of my insecurities, and I am so thankful we could work through it together. Marrying Albert was one of the first times I actually felt like someone was going to stick with me, and I didn't know how hard it would be to accept that at first.

SETTLING IN, BRANCHING OUT

*W*ithin three years after graduating from cosmetology school, I had settled into my new role behind the chair and had worked hard to build up my clientele. I had also taken a step to pursue something in the hair world beyond the salon. I had auditioned and been accepted as an educator for the men's grooming company, American Crew. This meant that I would continue to work behind the chair as well as teach local classes for Crew.

I was thrilled! I couldn't wait to teach haircutting and product knowledge to my fellow stylists and barbers. I began to teach classes in salons and barber shops across the state. When I wasn't teaching, I was busy behind the chair in the salon.

As fate would have it, I ended up giving a haircut to a woman that I would end up asking out on a date. In the hair world that isn't something you are supposed to do! The joke is that if you ask a client out, you end up losing them as a client either way. You either stay together and lose them as a paying client, or things don't work out and you still lose them! In this case we stayed together, and yes, I lost her as a paying client.

As we began dating, it was one of the first times that I started to consider what the future might look like. I had been through several relationships, and now I started to wonder what the next stage in my life would bring. What would a long-term relationship look like?

I knew I wanted to be married at some point. I also hoped to become a father someday. Dating Kim brought those thoughts to the front of my mind. I could think about them and start to see the possibilities. Kim came from a devout Catholic family, which made things even more comfortable since I had been Catholic for ten years at that point. We dated for a year, and then I gathered the courage to ask her to marry me. Leading up to that, I had shared my past with Kim and explained the events that had taken place. This also included explaining why I wasn't close with my parents. Kim understood and accepted where I was with things.

As we started to prepare for the wedding, I had to decide on a guest list from my side. I bring that up only because when you aren't close with your family you start to realize how limited your personal guest list is! The groomsmen were made up of my closest friends, and my "best man" was actually a "best woman," as one of my closest childhood friends, Gerilyn, filled the role. We had a traditional Catholic wedding, followed by an action-packed reception, and with that, the next stage of my life had begun. I was now married and had started to build my own family.

$\mathcal{P}$

AND THEN FATHERHOOD
CHANGED THINGS

A few years after our wedding, we purchased a home and stayed busy renovating and preparing for the next stages of our marriage. It didn't take long before we moved to the next family milestone, which involved discussing when we would try to become parents. We felt like we were at as good of a point as any and decided to see what would happen.

The green light was lit, and we became fully engrossed with researching everything related to babies. I went down the rabbit hole of reading books and asking friends about their experiences with parenting. I looked up everything I could find on childbirth and parenting. The information seemed endless!

After all of the reading, discussions, and multiple pregnancy tests, the "+" sign magically appeared and we knew that Kim was pregnant. The realization that I was going to become a father hit me in a very big way. It was no longer "what if" and instead became "we are."

After the excitement had subsided, it dawned on me that this was very real. I would soon become a father to a child and would end up stepping into a role that I wasn't sure I could handle. As I pondered this, I thought of my role models. My initial response was to think of the role my father had played in my upbringing. What were the most impactful moments he had shared with me? What lessons did I walk away with? I would ask myself those questions over and over, hoping I would be able to produce a list of those life lessons. It wasn't as easy as I thought to do that.

Meanwhile, we continued to prepare our house for the new arrival in every way imaginable. We painted the baby's room, bought every product under the sun that we thought would help us, and then waited anxiously. The big water-breaking moment didn't happen because we ended up having to schedule our delivery to avoid any health issues. We were in our due date range, so scheduling the birth made things even easier. After all the talking, preparing, and worrying, our big moment had arrived.

I will never forget the moment I saw my son, Sam, for the first time. The delivery of a child is a miracle to me, and I was transfixed as my son was making his way "out." Our doctor looked at me and said, "Now would be a good time for a photo if you would like one." I quickly grabbed my camera and took a photo of him holding Sam up mere moments after he came into our world. Truly amazing.

From that moment on, my life had changed permanently. After an exciting and sleepless night in the hospital we were allowed to pack up and head home. I remember walking into our living room and putting our son's car seat on the floor. Then Kim and I sat on the couch and gazed at Sam, who was fast asleep. The house was completely quiet, and as we looked around, we both said the same thing: "*Now* what do we do?"

You have probably heard the saying, "Children don't come with an instruction book." That statement is true, and at that moment I realized the life lessons I had learned would now be put to the test. I also knew I would be writing my own lessons along the way.

With the birth of Sam, I found myself facing a strange moment. I wanted to share the great news about my newborn child with family and friends. This would also mean visits by those same people. The visits did occur with Kim's family, as well as our friends, but our initial contact with my parents was limited to phone calls. My dad would eventually make his way to our home to see Sam, but not my mother. We were indeed separated, and this was part of it. Dad visited early on, but he had very little contact after that. My mother would eventually see Sam when we brought him over to see her. It didn't feel good to have these interactions play out this way. It was the opposite of what you would want to see from your parents. At times, it was embarrassing. I felt bad to have Kim see them act that way, and I didn't want anyone else to know how things were with my parents.

I found myself wondering about Melyssa after we brought Sam home from the hospital. She would have been part of this celebration. This was a moment that we would have celebrated together as siblings. It hurt to think about it. I wondered where she was and if she was starting her own family now. Surely by now she would have started a family? How could I be at such an exciting stage of life and not have any family members to share it with? It was a stark reminder of how far apart we were.

M

BABIES AND THE CALL

Albert and I welcomed our first baby on April 14, 2001. Our beautiful daughter Olivia came into our world, and I was now entering a chapter of my life that I was scrambling to figure out. It was a moment that I will never forget. After everything I had been through, I was now a mother holding my baby. I kept wondering how I was going to raise her and if I could do all the things that a good mother was supposed to do. It was overwhelming at first, because I was trying to figure out how to get into a routine with my daughter, but in the back of my head I knew I needed to go back to work soon. I started questioning how I would raise her and manage a work schedule. I wanted to step down from managing the salon so I could concentrate on doing hair for my clients and also have more time with my daughter.

The owners of the salon told me that if I stepped down, I would have to transfer to a different Hair Cuttery location, which would most likely be in the mall. That meant I would have to change my hours to line up with the mall's hours, which was not appealing. I couldn't believe they would want to transfer me out that easily. It didn't feel like the work I had been doing was valued, so I decided to leave that very day. One of my coworkers told me to go to the Hair Gallery, which was a booth rental salon. My coworker made the call to her friend who owned the salon, and he told me to come over.

I called all of my regular clients immediately and told them I had moved. I couldn't believe I had made such a crazy decision, but it turned out to be one of the best decisions I had ever made.

Leaving a salon where I was a stylist and becoming a "booth renter" transformed me into an independent business owner. I had to manage my expenses and make every decision from a business owner's perspective. That was a big change from having someone else handling all of that!

Over the next few years, I made a few more moves before settling in at Sola Salon, where I have my own studio with a full clientele. My clients have been wonderful and have stayed with me throughout the moves in my career. Having my own studio gave me much more flexibility to be with my kids so I could be the best mom I could be to them.

Shortly after Olivia's second birthday we welcomed Albert IV, who was born on July 4, 2003. I now had a daughter and a son in addition to running a full-time business. Life had truly changed, and I felt like I had hit a point where things had really fallen into a good place. My life felt complete. Well, almost complete. I still felt like there was one missing piece. Patrick kept popping into my mind from time to time and I couldn't shake a few questions out of my head about him.

I was reading a book called *Suzanne's Diary for Nicholas*, and for some reason it made me think of Patrick. I wondered where he was and what he was doing. Had he gotten married? Did he have any children? Where was he at this stage in his life?

I shared my thoughts with a coworker who told me to just call him. It seemed simple, but I was nervous as I thought about our previous encounter when he hadn't seemed to want to have anything to do with me.

One night I decided to call Patrick's dad, Earl, to ask him for Patrick's phone number. I hadn't talked to Earl since I graduated from high school. When I called him, he told me that he had remarried and was now living in Charlotte, too! At one point he had worked down the road from a salon I had worked in!

Earl gave me Patrick's phone number, and I called him immediately. I was so scared, but this time our conversation was different. He was excited to talk to me, and we immediately started to share stories about our families and what we were doing. Our conversation flowed naturally and felt good. I was happy to find out that he was still doing hair and had also become an educator for American Crew.

Patrick told me that he was married and that he and his wife had one child and another one on the way. I shared my story about my marriage and kids as well. We had so much to catch up on that our phone call lasted for a long time. We ended the call by promising never to be apart again. My heart was so happy, and I couldn't believe how well things were going!

Near the end of the call, Patrick decided to come to Charlotte for a visit. That sounded great, and I mentioned that I would be in Nebraska during the summer. We both decided my visit to Nebraska would give us a chance to kick things off. It would allow him to spend time with his wife before their second baby was born, and we would talk again prior to the trip.

After that first call, Patrick and I continued to call each other as often as we could, and we kept sharing more details about our past. We wanted to rebuild our relationship and to find out what had happened to each other along the way. It felt so great to know we had reconnected, and at the same time we were realizing that we had so much more to share to make things seem whole again.

$\mathcal{P}$

THE CALL

It was a normal night by all accounts, and Kim and I were winding down since it was 10:45 p.m. Sam was asleep, which was great news since he was one year old and Kim was halfway through her second pregnancy and was tired and lying down next to me. We had flipped through various TV channels and started watching the Tonight Show when the phone rang.

Kim answered the phone and then motioned that it was for me. After I put the phone to my ear and said hello, I heard, "Hi Pat, this is Melyssa." I instantly sat up in bed and tried to understand what was happening. Just listening to her say those words hit me fast and hard. Was this really happening? Yes, it was, and now I was trying to process a million thoughts at once.

As I sat in bed and talked with Melyssa, I kept telling myself to remain calm. That may sound stupid because there was no pressure involved, but I didn't want to blow this. I didn't know if I would get another chance to speak with her, and I wanted this connection to last. What I couldn't figure out was how, and why, this was happening in the first place. I finally asked what had led her to reach out. Melyssa answered by telling me about a book she had read. The book didn't follow our storyline, but certain parts resonated with her enough that she started thinking about me more and more. After sharing what she had been thinking with a friend, she was encouraged to search me out. She then went for it and called.

After that, we dove in and started asking each other questions. We proceeded to tell each other about everything that was going on in our lives. Words just flew out of my mouth! I couldn't believe it! I was talking on the phone with my sister, and if I told you that it was the greatest phone call I've ever had, I wouldn't be lying!

As we went back and forth with our questions and answers, the comfort level continued to grow. We had a blast, and as we were getting ready to wind down our call, we had a moment where we weren't sure what would happen next. Melyssa told me that she was planning to come to Nebraska in July to see her family, and she asked if we could spend some time together. We would have to wait eight months to see each other, but that was okay because we would have many more phone conversations before seeing each other in person.

With one phone call, our lives had shifted in ways that we had never expected! That call gave me an emotional boost that I could never describe fully. It was a dream come true, and I couldn't wait to see what would happen next!

P
ADDING ON

In December of 2005, my sweet daughter Lily came into the world. Kim and I were thrilled because we had hoped to have children who could grow up close in age. Having a boy and a girl was great! It was fun to see the differences between the two as Lily started to grow. As I watched the two of them, I realized I was starting to compare myself to where my parents were when they had two kids. I would think about what I was doing and wonder how my parents would have reacted. I would find myself questioning whether I was reacting in a different way than they might have when they were raising me and my sisters. Was I responding similarly? Was I making better decisions? Now that I was a parent, were my decisions and actions influenced by what I had grown up seeing and hearing?

I thought about my parents so often that it started to bother me. I had decided that when I got married, I was going to do things differently as a husband and father. I had seen my family torn apart by terrible decisions, in addition to watching a failed marriage crumble in front of me. I wanted to do the opposite of what my parents had done.

Kim came from a close-knit family. We lived a few blocks from her parents and only a few houses away from one of her sisters. The entire family was in close contact daily. When it came to family gatherings for holidays, birthdays, or any special occasion, we would be at each other's homes.

The closeness of Kim's family dynamic took a bit for me to get accustomed to. In a way, it was what I had always wanted to be part of. I had now married into the scenario that I had envisioned as being the family that I never had. In another way, I had become so independent that it made me slightly uncomfortable to always be among family members. I had to adjust to the fact they had grown up this way and now I had married right into the middle of it. I didn't realize how much of an adjustment that would be for me.

Kim's family wasn't doing anything wrong. In fact, it was just the opposite. They were an amazing family who supported each other through thick and thin. Did they have disagreements or fights? Sure, but that is part of life. They always worked through their conflicts and continued to love and support each other. They were a "normal" family, and that's what was so great about them. I was the one who had to adjust to this.

At family get-togethers Kim knew that after a certain amount of time I would find a reason to go home. This became a pattern, but I didn't realize it at first. When I finally did recognize the pattern, I started to ask myself why I would default to that action. Why did I hit that point where I wanted to leave? I came to realize it was because I needed to be home and be in my space with my kids. I felt comfortable there. I had grown accustomed to taking care of myself and pushing away the family that I had. Being independent allowed me to control who was close to me. It was a defense mechanism. Being in "my space" was safe and allowed me to relax.

As much as I felt like I had a new life and was doing things my way, I also was coming to realize I had not resolved the issues from my past. My discomfort was starting to surface, and it would cause tension when we discussed it.

Those first few years were a blur as we kept busy with our kids and family gatherings. It didn't take long before Sam was heading into preschool, with Lily not far behind. It was fun to watch our children interact and grow quickly, but it was also a distraction from the fact that I was troubled. Kim and I had normal ups and downs as a married couple, and now that we had kids some of those tensions rose higher. The troubled feeling that I had wasn't centered around normal marital arguments, though. It went deeper than that. My feelings about my family of origin had been buried and were starting to resurface. It was easy to distance myself from those feelings when I was busy with the kids. I had very little interaction with my parents, which made it easier to keep my thoughts focused elsewhere as well.

During the first years of our marriage my mother's health had started to decline, and I started to get calls to help in different ways. Actually, Kim helped in more ways than I did at first. Kim was a Registered Nurse who had worked in the I.C.U. of a hospital. My mother knew that and now saw her as an option for help.

One of the health issues my mother struggled with was multiple sclerosis. At the time, she had several symptoms of MS, and one of the ways to keep flare-ups from occurring was to receive a daily injection. The injections were designed to be administered by the patient, but my mother said that she couldn't do it. Instead, she wanted Kim to do it. Kim was a great caregiver and offered to teach my mother how to give herself the daily shot. She even tried to practice with her by using fruit to demonstrate how to insert the needle. None of the practice made any difference and my mother insisted that Kim give her the injection. This created a new level of stress as Kim went to my mother's home weekly to do this.

The injections helped for a while, but my mother's health continued to spiral downward as she stopped taking care of herself. She was losing weight due to poor eating habits, and her self-care was minimal. At one point, Kim entered my mother's house and noticed a strong smell as she got closer to Beth. Kim instantly knew that it was urine. She helped Beth get into the bathtub to get cleaned up, but after she was done, Kim couldn't get her out of the tub. An ambulance had to be called to get my mother out of the tub and back into bed. She had developed a urinary tract infection due to her inability to get to the bathroom, and now that had to be addressed.

Eventually Kim stopped giving my mother the injections, and a visiting nurse took over the duties. Watching all of this unfold started to weigh on me. I had multiple thoughts that bounced around in my head at any given moment. I hated to see my mother suffer and decline. At the same time, I was irritated by her unwillingness to care for herself and her lack of appreciation for everyone who was helping her.

I also struggled with thoughts about the past. I didn't have answers to many of my questions, and I felt like my mother owed me some explanations. My mixed emotions would stay with me as her health problems intensified and then subsided over the next few years. When her condition was stable, everything would calm down and it was easy to revert to holding her at a distance. Then her health would deteriorate again, and I would start to wonder if she was taking a turn for the worse.

At one point my mother was hospitalized and I visited her. I remember standing in her room and initiating an awkward conversation. It was awkward in the sense that it was a basic back-and-forth about how she was feeling and how the kids were, but it was very forced and superficial. I knew I was on the verge of leaving, so I finally asked her a question that I had waited years to ask. I was hoping to get an answer that would put my mind at ease. I wanted to gain insight into why she had made the decision that had broken our family apart.

I said, "I just want to know one thing. Why did you decide that having Melyssa leave was the answer?"

My mother looked at me for a minute and then quietly said, "I thought it was the best thing to do for the family."

I stared at her, shook my head, and said "Goodbye" as I turned and walked out of the room.

That was it. There wasn't going to be a revelation. I wasn't going to finally hear the hidden truth behind her actions. She thought it was the best thing for the family. That was all I was going to get, and now I would have to figure out how to live with that.

$\mathcal{P}$
THE REUNION

Melyssa and I had spoken on the phone several times since her first call. We shared stories about our past and our family life, and then made plans for her upcoming visit to Nebraska. The Fourth of July was coming up soon, and she planned on visiting the Brandt family during the holiday. She invited Kim and me to spend time with the Brandts in a smaller town just outside of Omaha. They would be having a cookout next to a lake and would have plenty of food and activities for everyone involved.

As we drove to meet Melyssa, I felt a sense of excitement mixed with a basket of butterflies in my stomach. We had made good progress during our phone conversations, and now I wondered how we would react when we were actually facing each other. I also was nervous about meeting the Brandt family. Melyssa had described them to me, but I couldn't picture the group in my mind. When Melyssa described the cookout, it sounded like a large group would be gathering.

We made our way to the lake and found the spot where the group had gathered. It was apparent right away that quite a few people were attending the cookout. People were bunched around picnic tables, kids were chasing each other, and several people were standing or sitting next to the lake as a group was swimming.

Kim and I grabbed Sam and Lily and our things, then walked toward a group close to the food. As we approached, Melyssa shouted: "Patrick! Hey, you guys made it!"

I saw my sister walking toward us, smiling from ear to ear. I put my bags down and we hugged for the first time in twenty-four years. We held onto each other for a minute and then pulled away to look at each other. I was staring at my sister, and I was trying to take it all in. I had dreamed of this day but had thought it would never happen.

I stepped back to introduce Kim and the kids, and Melyssa gave each of them a huge hug. After that, several members of the Brandt family came over and introduced themselves. I felt slightly overwhelmed as I met more and more of them. There were so many people at this gathering! I wasn't sure who was who and how they were related to each other. Melyssa laughed and told me not to worry about it because I would get to know them later.

The rest of the day was spent eating, meeting family members, and watching my kids play. Melyssa and I didn't get a lot of one-on-one time, but it still felt great to be together.

Since it was July, it was quite warm out. Our kids were still very young and they needed to go to bed. We gathered our gear and loaded it into the car, then I made my way back to Melyssa to say goodbye. We made sure to tell each other, "Goodbye for now, and I will see you soon!"

We hugged, and then I turned and headed to the car. The drive home was quiet because Kim and I were both worn out.

My heart was full, though. Things had finally come full circle. A part of me that had been lost had been found. All I could do was smile as I thought about how great it had been to see Melyssa again.

Patrick and Melyssa, The reunion! Fremont, Nebraska, 2005

P

TURNS OUT THERAPY
HELPS

As time passed, the tension in our house grew as Kim and I argued continually. The arguments could start over any small thing and then build. Sam and Lily were young enough that we could keep them away from our discussions, but that wouldn't work forever.

My thoughts swirled until I started to feel out of control. I knew I needed help but wasn't sure where to turn. The idea of getting therapy was brought up, and I decided to pursue it.

Finding a therapist is interesting. You can start with a referral from a trusted source or you can take a chance. I took a chance.

As with all therapy sessions, it takes a while to unpack things and get into a groove as a level of trust builds. Reaching that trust level was tough for me, but we eventually broke through. Part of the therapy involved taking medication to give me a boost. I will give the medication credit for helping to lift me out of the melancholy that I would frequently drop into. In addition, the therapy helped me to sort my thoughts out and address them in ways that I hadn't attempted before.

Over time I had chosen to bury my issues internally and push them back as they periodically rose to the surface.

It takes a lot of energy to suppress unwanted thoughts and feelings. I had carried them with me throughout my life, and the weight had continued to drag me down. Of course, as my therapist and I dug into my issues it wasn't hard to see that the events of the past were playing a key role in my current struggles. I had not truly dealt with the issues effectively. My anger toward my parents was just below the surface and would rise whenever something started to frustrate me. That didn't help when the frustration I was feeling could have been solved rather simply.

I also realized that I struggled with shame over what had happened in my family of origin. I didn't want anyone to know what my parents had done. It was embarrassing, and I didn't want to be judged. Feelings of shame would throw me off and eventually bring my mood down until a level of depression would set in.

My relationship with Kim was affected by my internal struggles. My mood would dictate my reactions, and I would get into an argument with Kim. Even though those issues were influencing my mood, I knew that I should have reacted better. The past shouldn't be an excuse for behaving badly in the present. Everyone goes through difficulties that can affect how they deal with things. That being said, I hadn't done the work that was needed to deal with my issues. As a result, my moods were affected and I was reacting in a way that pushed back at everyone around me.

The therapy sessions helped me to address two key issues that were affecting me, one being my parents, and the other my marriage. Both had to be dealt with if I was going to move forward.

The issues I had with my mother were coming to a head because her health was declining at a steady rate. I had many conversations where the statement, "If you don't make peace with her before she dies, you will regret it forever" was said to me. I wrestled with that comment a lot. People were implying that if I didn't forgive her before she died, then I would carry the guilt with me for the rest my life.

I ended up meeting with a Catholic priest from my parish. I explained the back-and-forth debate that was raging within me. Should I have this conversation with her, or should I accept what happened and forgive her? He offered a suggestion that gave me peace of mind. He asked me if I knew about the Catholic prayers for the deceased or dying. I said yes, but I was unsure of how those prayers were going to solve my issues. He went on to explain that the prayers we say for the deceased aren't just made in remembrance of that person. They also allow us to continue to pray about any unresolved issues we have with that person.

The priest said, "Patrick, I know everyone has told you to make peace before she passes. The truth is you probably can't, based on what you have told me. Instead, lean into these prayers after she passes and use that as an opportunity to show grace and find that peace."

When he said that, it made sense to me. Part of the weight I had been carrying had been lifted. I knew I wasn't finished healing, but I felt like I had a found a way to cope. It was some of the best advice that I have ever received.

P
MOVING OUT

After many therapy sessions and endless conversations with Kim, I decided it was time to move out. The sessions with my therapist had helped me to understand the main issues that I had been struggling with, but it had also shed light on the fact that I had not been dealing with them at all. The anger I had toward my parents had built up throughout my life and was now surfacing when I would react to Kim. This hurt her immensely, and I hated that it had done so.

Over time, I had grown distant in our relationship and the arguments we were having built up defensive walls for both of us. I tried to work through the distance I had created, but it wasn't helping. My marriage was in trouble, and I knew deep down it wasn't going to be resolved.

I searched for an apartment and tried to figure out how things were going to work. I moved into an apartment 15 minutes away, and Kim and I established a split parenting schedule while the divorce process was underway. The first weeks in my apartment felt very surreal. After seven years of marriage and living in a home that we had worked on together and filled with our family, I was now in an apartment and the silence was deafening. I knew that this was the path I needed to take, yet I doubted myself multiple times a day. The doubt was a natural response because I had uprooted myself from everything that should have been comfortable.

The doubts continued to creep in but were accompanied by realizations that I was doing what I needed to do. I knew that I needed to move forward and find some peace within myself.

Everyone always asks, "What happened?" when a couple goes through a divorce. People tend to look for a "smoking gun" so they can attach that to the situation and justify what happened. In this case, there was no smoking gun. No one had cheated. There wasn't a drinking or gambling problem. There weren't any physical altercations. It all came down to me and the fact that our relationship wasn't working. Kim was a great mother and wife, but in the end, it just wasn't a good fit, especially as I continued to work on things within myself.

Divorce is never easy, regardless of the reason. As I settled into my new routine, my friends stepped in and helped to fill in the time between the days when I had my kids. When you go through a divorce, you suddenly notice that some of your friends "take sides." I get it, but it also is a great reminder of who is in your corner when things get rough.

My sister and my close friends continued to lift me up when I needed it. The time with my kids was also a huge boost. The kids were young enough that the transition became their new normal. They were four and two years old at the time, and they adapted quickly. I made sure that Kim would keep the house and everything that the kids were familiar with so they could carry on their regular routine as much as possible. The biggest change for them was coming to Dad's house and exploring and playing in a new space. This worked well because they thought it was a fun place to hang out!

During this period of time, my mother's health continued to decline. She was receiving daily visits from a home care nurse, but her condition had not improved. We also began to understand more about what she was facing. It turned out there was more affecting her than the MS that she had been battling. She had been diagnosed with cancer that started as a melanoma and then spread to other parts of her body. A cruel irony is that her physical state with MS had masked some symptoms and allowed the cancer to go undetected for a while. Now it had gone from a skin issue to an internal one. The question was how far it had gone and what the prognosis would be.

After several tests and scans, it became clear that my mother's prospects for recovering weren't good. The cancer had spread into her lymph system and had gotten into a few organs. At this stage chemotherapy wasn't a good option because she had become so weak. Her health was failing, and it was a waiting game now. Things would soon shift to a home hospice situation, and I knew I would have to face things head on.

$\mathcal{P}$
COMING TO TERMS

I was sitting in a conference room attending a meeting when I received the call. At this time in my career, I had taken a job with a beauty supply company and had more of a corporate position within the hair industry. It was a meeting with a hair brand, and we were discussing one of the key ingredients in their new shampoo. Bamboo was the featured ingredient, and as we discussed the performance strengths my cell phone vibrated with a call. I got up and walked out of the room as I said hello. I immediately heard "You need to come now" from my aunt. By this time my mother had been moved to a hospice facility and we knew that things could shift quickly at any moment.

I rushed back into the conference room and told my boss that I needed to leave. The bamboo shampoo would have to wait. As I arrived at the hospice center and walked into her room, I saw my Aunt Kate and my grandmother, Sylva. My younger sister, Dere, would arrive soon after. We hadn't seen each other in years, and now we were standing together at our mother's deathbed. The entire scene felt awkward, but there was no time to think about our discomfort.

My mother was on a bed in the middle of the room. It was midday, and she was still coherent. We were able to converse to some degree. She was slower with her responses and her speech was not strong, but she was still responding to questions and could answer fairly well. Being able to ask her questions and get responses was what made this part of the day feel strange to me.

I had received a call telling me to get there fast. That shifted me into a panic mode. However, after I arrived, I was able to talk with her. I started to relax, and it gave me some hope that maybe this was a false alarm. I started to think that she might have had a bad morning, and they got worried and gave me a call. I was still tense, though, and kept analyzing every move or answer she would make. I also quizzed my aunt and grandmother as well as any nurse that came in. I was looking for anything that would clue me in about why they felt this might be the day. No one could give me a definitive answer.

We were in a hospice facility, and they were used to dealing with these situations, so it made me believe that they knew something was coming. Because of that I tried to stay focused every minute. The afternoon passed quickly, with nurses coming and going as the family watched every move or sound that my mother would make. As the time ticked by, it was apparent that her condition was worsening. There were moments where we knew she was feeling pain based on a facial expression, followed by a moan, which would prompt us to reach out to the nurse who checked her pain medication.

I tried to stay by her side and talk to her as much as I could. At one point I knew that if I wanted to make sure that she completely understood what I was saying, I had better say whatever I needed to say soon. I wanted her to hear me and to be able to respond.

As the hours passed, I kept thinking about all of the anger, sadness, and other pent-up feelings that had led to this moment. We were only two feet apart, and her life was about to end. There was no more time for arguments or questions. I knew that whatever feelings I had left would have to walk out of the room with me, and I would have to contend with them later. At that moment I wanted her to know one thing. I said, "Mom, I want you to know something. I love you."

I waited for a moment, and then she said, "I know. I love you too." She gave my hand a light squeeze, and I felt a sense of relief wash over me. She had heard me, and it had registered. I needed her to know because it might give her more peace. It was for both of us, though. We both needed to be uplifted at that moment.

As the afternoon shifted into early evening, her condition declined rapidly. Her breathing was becoming more labored, and waves of pain were washing over her. I looked at my mother and then at a nurse who was checking on things, and I knew we were getting close. The nurse then stepped out and left the moment to our family. My aunt and grandmother sat down as Dere and I stood on each side of our mother. I looked at her and said, "You can quit fighting now. It's okay to let go. We are here with you, and it's okay to let go." I repeated that a few times, and then she inhaled deeply and then slowly exhaled one final time.

I stared down at her in disbelief and then slowly let go of her hand. It was over. A strange silence filled the room as we all took a breath and stepped back from the bed. We took a few moments to hug each other and compose ourselves.

The nurses took over shortly after that, and eventually we quietly went our separate ways. I made a few phone calls to friends as I drove home, and I recall walking into my apartment and pouring myself a cocktail. My head was spinning as I tried to process what had happened. I quickly finished the glass and shuffled to bed where I finally drifted off, knowing that my life had just shifted in a very big way.

M

THE END OF ONE CHAPTER?

I soon learned that Patrick's mom, Beth, was very sick with cancer and that she didn't have much time left. I also learned they didn't have a close relationship, but I knew that he was hurting so much about his feelings towards her. All I could do was listen and try to be there for him. I was learning a lot about his relationship with his parents, and as I began to understand their past, I realized why they weren't close now.

It made me so sad for him. Patrick really had no family. They barely spoke to each other and now he was trying to deal with the fact that Beth was in poor condition. I was so thankful I was there for him.

One day I asked Patrick if he would be okay if I sent Beth flowers. He was fine with it as long as I felt okay with doing it. I remember writing the following message to Beth on the card: "I forgive you. You did what you thought was right. Sincerely, Melyssa."

I wanted her to know that I was okay, and I wanted her to know that I had forgiven her.

Days later I received a call from Patrick, and he told me that Beth had passed away.

I didn't know what to say other than to tell him that I was there for him. There were various extended family members around him, but I knew none of them were close.

Regardless of the rough state of Patrick's relationship with Beth, I knew he was still coming to terms with the reality of losing a parent. I hoped he could see that he had my support even from a distance and that he could find peace.

STEPS FORWARD

During the weeks and months after my mother passed away, I found myself trying to reconcile some of my feelings about her as well as acknowledging what had happened in the past. In addition, I was finding it difficult to shake the images from her final day at the hospice center. Those images were not the ones that I wanted to have in my head when I thought about her. If you have ever attended a funeral that had an open casket, the body in the casket may not have resembled the person you knew. Well, being with my mother when she passed away took that feeling up a notch. She was very ill, and physically she was at the worst stage of her life. I have often gone back to old photos just to try to put a different image in my head.

I was also coming to grips with the feelings around my relationship with her. As I processed everything that had happened, I found amazing support from my friends and sister. They showed up when needed and gave me space when it was called for. I also dug in at work, and I made sure that the time with my kids was well spent.

As the following year unfolded, my divorce worked its way through the legal system. It was an "amicable" divorce, but it still took time to go through the legal formalities. Eventually I had to go into a courtroom, answer a few questions, and sign the divorce papers. The legal process took about a year.

While my divorce was under way I went on a few dates, but nothing came of them. I knew I wanted to be in a relationship, but after a year of being on my own, I wasn't sure if I wanted to get involved with anyone. I went out with friends from work, and that helped to fill most of my social time.

I worked in a company where my role had me crossing over between several departments. Because of the crossover I was able to get to know quite a few people within the company. Several of the situations that I had to contend with meant working with our customer service department to resolve issues. The customer service team had to make people happy as they shipped orders or fixed issues. They dealt with customers and employees over the phone, and I was able to watch some of their interactions in person. In doing so, I could see when their smile was projected through the phone. It sounds funny, but it is true that you can project your smile and attitude through a phone conversation, and it makes all the difference in the world!

In that busy department I met Jenny. It is not often that you meet someone who radiates positivity. She smiled constantly, and her face lit up as she spoke. Her outfits were always on point, and she shined wherever she was. To be honest I felt intimidated as I first got to know her. She didn't try to intimidate me, but I felt that she was on a higher level than I was. Over time we became friends and were able to joke and laugh as we interacted. I had thought about asking her out but didn't think that I would have a shot.

Over time, I gradually found the courage to ask Jenny out, but before I had the chance to follow through, I blew it. I was walking down the hallway at work and noticed Jenny standing in the doorway of my friend's office. They were talking, and as

I approached, I realized that Jenny was crying. At that point I tried to insert humor in an effort to "help." I walked in with a big grin and said, "Hey, there's no crying in baseball!" I quickly realized that my Tom Hanks impression from *A League of Their Own* did not land the way I had intended. I glanced at my friend, who gave me a look that said, "Shut up, you idiot!" Jenny left and moved quickly down the hall.

I sat down in my friend's office and said, "I swear I was just trying to lighten the mood!" My friend informed me that Jenny had just gone through a breakup. My attempt at humor had failed miserably, and so had my prospects of asking her out. I walked away and immediately tried to figure out how to apologize.

Luckily for me, Jenny realized that I had not known about her breakup and was merely trying to lighten things up. We worked past the crying episode, and I eventually mustered the courage to ask her out. We ended up going out on a first date and having a ton of fun together, and after that it was off to the races. Fifteen years later, we are married and have grown our family to include two beautiful daughters, in addition to my oldest son and daughter. What happened after our first date was important to me on many levels. During that period things started to click for me personally and professionally, and my sister and I uncovered a lot about our past.

NEW BEGINNINGS AND HARD REALITIES

As I entered my second marriage, I knew that I wanted Jenny to have a full understanding of my past and where I was at that moment. She deserved that. I was divorced and had two young children. I had come from a broken family, and it was "messy."

Jenny was open about her family life as well. Her parents divorced when she was quite young and her mother remarried, which added two stepsisters to Jenny's world. A member of her immediate family was struggling with addiction, and I saw the impact of that experience as well. To sum up, each of us brought our own issues to the family that we were creating.

As we prepared for our wedding, we decided to find a church and a pastor that could help us start off on the right foot. We found a church that we liked and set up a meeting. We walked into the church for our meeting with excitement and sat down to talk with the head pastor. He asked us the obvious first questions just to understand the timing of the wedding, and then he asked about our history. Jenny and I proceeded to unpack each of our personal family stories, and as we did, the look on his face grew increasingly troubled. He finally told us that based on our family histories we would need quite a bit of counseling to deal with the past if we wanted to have a successful marriage. To say that we were shocked by his comment would have been an understatement. We left and walked to our car silently.

After we sat down in the car, Jenny began to cry. I asked her what she was feeling, and she told me she felt judged for our families' past, and in turn it made her feel terrible. I agreed and drove home quickly.

The next day, I emailed the pastor and told him how he had made both of us feel. I also asked him if that was how he and his church approached all newcomers and if his lack of acceptance was truly a Christian approach. Shouldn't he welcome newcomers and strive to be non-judgmental? His suggestion of undergoing counseling prior to marriage prep seemed ridiculous to me. We hadn't walked in to ask for help. We had shared openly as he asked questions. We had nothing to hide. I let him know how dismayed I had been by his comments. To his credit, he responded with an apology. He stated that he would reevaluate his approach as he moved forward, and he said he would understand if we didn't come back.

We didn't go back to that pastor. Instead, we received an excellent recommendation from a trusted friend, Craig Wilkins. We set up a meeting with a pastor named Gavin Johnson and sat down with him between church services on a Sunday morning. Jenny and I cut straight to the chase and told him about our recent experience with the other pastor. We then quickly explained who we were and gave a brief overview of our past. I said, "If you can deal with us as we are, then we would love to work with you."

He looked at us and said, "You are right here, and that is what matters to me. Your past is the past, and if you are committed to moving forward with each other, then that is what I accept." With a smile and a handshake, we had met someone who would go on to be a family friend as well as our pastor. During the weeks prior to our wedding, we met with Gavin and his wife regularly. Our conversations with them were very helpful to us.

When the big day finally arrived, it was amazing! Our families and friends were there, and having Melyssa in the wedding party was one of the greatest feelings in the world. Seeing her, along with my brother-in-law, niece, and nephew, dancing with Sam and Lily and all of our friends was one of the best experiences I have ever had.

Wedding day! Jenny and Melyssa with Patrick.
One of the happiest days of my life! 2011

Conversely, our wedding day also proved to be a very painful day personally. I had invited my father, who was living in upstate New York. He had remarried and his wife had family in the area where they settled. He had sent an RSVP back acknowledging that he would be attending. Even though we weren't close, it still meant something to me to have him witness my wedding. He would also be able to see his grandchildren, Sam and Lily. I felt like it was an opportunity to show him where I was in life and how proud I was of my family. I wanted him to see the happiness that I was experiencing. I truly wanted him to see what his son had done and how I was surrounded by amazing people. Those thoughts didn't last long, though. Two weeks before the wedding, he informed me that he wouldn't be able to come after all. He told me he was dealing with a medical issue that prohibited him from traveling. I was stunned as I listened to the news. I took it in and then told him that I understood and he should do whatever he needed to do to get back to full health.

After our phone conversation ended, I stared out the window for a few minutes. I felt disappointed, hurt, and angry. I also felt embarrassed. My father wouldn't be there, and I instantly thought of people asking why he wasn't at the wedding. I had gone back to where I had started with him.

I exhaled deeply and then went to find Jenny to tell her about the conversation. She was disappointed and aware that I felt let down. Even though it was disappointing news, I wasn't completely shocked. I had not seen my father for years, and our only contact during that time had been an occasional phone call that typically lasted only a few minutes. He had seen my children twice before he moved out of state, so they truly didn't know who he was. The ties between my father and me were very limited.

After Jenny and I talked, I tried to shake off my disappointment and shift my thinking toward having a great wedding. As I mentioned before, the wedding was fantastic and in the two weeks afterwards we continued to ride a blissful high. That feeling continued until I received a call from my dad. He left a voice message informing me that he was "Having a great time on my trip!" I was confused and called Melyssa to ask her if she knew what trip he was talking about. She did some digging on social media and found out that he and his wife had taken a vacation two weeks after my wedding—the same wedding that he had told me he couldn't attend due to his health. Somehow during those two weeks he had made a strong enough recovery to go on vacation and have a "great time."

My father had chosen a vacation over attending my wedding. Instead of watching me get married and celebrating the occasion with his grandchildren, he had been enjoying "a great time" with his wife. Unfortunately, this choice was yet another in a string that had come to represent the current state of our relationship as father and son. Our relationship was broken, and there was no going back.

Within the years after Jenny and I got married, I found out that my father and his wife had traveled multiple times to visit members of her family who lived one hour away from Omaha. I acquired that information during a random phone call from my dad. Each time I heard that he had been nearby but had not visited or called, it felt like a punch to the gut.

There is great pain in knowing that my father didn't value our relationship enough to take an active role in my life. Not just my life, but my children's lives as well. There are no calls on a birthday or at Christmas for them or for me. My children don't have a relationship with him. They have grown up not knowing about him, and in some ways so did I.

P

SO, WHAT ABOUT YOUR OTHER SISTER?

I have been asked about my sister Dere periodically, and it's hard for me to figure out how to answer. Just to clarify, I am the oldest child in my family. Melyssa came next and was only two years younger than me. After that my parents were surprised to learn that my mother was able to get pregnant. That was when Dere, who is five years younger came into the picture. We had a normal bond between a five-year-old and a newborn, which is saying that a five-year-old typically thinks a baby is cute and then quickly moves on.

Five years can create quite a gap during middle and high school. When Melyssa was removed from our home, I was ten years old and Dere was five. After Melyssa was taken away, I withdrew emotionally from my family. If I had formed a bond with Dere, it was definitely strained after that. I wasn't going to get too close because if I did, I could get hurt just like I had been when Melyssa was taken away.

In other words, Dere and I were quite distant as we grew up. By the time I was in high school, I spent most of my time outside the house. After graduating from high school, I moved out. Dere and I hadn't had much contact before, and it certainly wasn't going to increase after I left.

Later, when our mother was in hospice care, Dere and I were together for her final day. Within days after my mother's passing, a lunch gathering was held for family and friends. That was the last time I saw my younger sister. Prior to my mother's passing, she had been living with my mother. They were close and stayed that way until her passing.

After my mother died, I found out that she had purchased a small life insurance policy that at one point had showed Dere and me as beneficiaries. At some point my name was removed. In the end, I didn't care about the money. It was about the principle involved. Our family was broken, and nothing was going to repair it. I was on the outside, and to be fair, I had no problem being there. As a matter of fact, I had chosen it. Nevertheless, it still hurt for a moment to know that my mother had removed my name from her insurance policy.

To this day, I have no contact with my youngest sister. We went on with our lives and not being close is an extension of the division that began when we were kids. People have criticized my lack of effort to change that, but it's okay with me. If they were closer to me, they would know that I had never formed a bond with Dere. I do not have any ill feelings toward her, and I hope she has a good life.

M
TWO DIFFERENT TYPES OF VISITS

After spending time with me and my family while I was in Nebraska, Patrick scheduled a flight to Charlotte and we were able to catch up and reconnect as brother and sister.

I learned about the pain he was going through and how my leaving the family had affected his relationship with his mom, dad, and sister. We had so much to talk about that it was almost overwhelming. Try packing twenty-four lost years into a weekend visit! We covered a lot of ground but also realized we would need even more time together to unpack everything. We enjoyed spending time with each other, and we ended the trip by making a commitment to take a yearly brother/sister trip every year after that. I am so thankful that I am part of his life now and that he has a loving family.

Over the next few years, we were able to experience some great family milestones together. Patrick asked me to be the godmother of his beautiful daughter, Lily, an invitation that I happily accepted! Later, when he became engaged to Jenny, he asked me to be in his second wedding. I felt so honored!

Those two events gave us a second chance to experience family events together. It was a great feeling, and I know how much they meant to both of us.

As time went by, Patrick and I talked about what happened during the time that we were apart. Gradually we started to ask each other more specific questions. As we did, we realized there were many details that each of us were learning about for the first time. One example was the fact that after Earl and I had spoken on the phone, he continued to call me periodically. He knew that we lived in the same city, so he asked if he could visit. I said yes, and we agreed to meet. I was more curious than anything, since it meant I would be able to meet his wife and see how their lives had been going.

Our visit was casual but became slightly uncomfortable when Earl started to revisit the past. He clearly felt sad as he spoke about it. He told me how sorry he was and saying that if he'd had the chance to do things over, he would have.

I stopped him and said, "But you didn't. You did what you thought was best." He began to cry as I told him that I have found happiness and have a loving family. It was a short visit, yet it answered some of my questions. He and his wife soon moved to New York state where they currently live.

Earl continued to call me, but I eventually cut off communication when I learned he had only met Patrick's kids twice. He had also chosen not to attend his only son's wedding because of a health issue. That decision might have been easier to accept if I hadn't seen a photo of Earl and his wife on vacation right after Patrick's wedding. Somehow, Earl had healed up quickly enough to travel. It bothers me that he never calls to wish Patrick a happy birthday, or on holidays, or even to acknowledge Patrick's kids. I just don't understand how he could treat his own child that way.

I learned a lot about Earl during this time. His second wife has a big, controlling personality, similar to how Beth was in his first marriage, and he does whatever she tells him to do. He doesn't have a backbone, and that has been proven over and again.

On a few of the phone calls he would say, "Hey Melyssa, this is Earl, your dad, or whatever you want to call me."

My response was quick: "You are not my dad. You gave that title up the day you let me go." That may sound harsh, but I have a dad now who has continued to show up in my life.

It has taken me a long time to stand up to Earl, but I can't stand how he treats his only son, and I will continue to stand up for myself and to defend Patrick.

$\mathcal{P}$
SO THEN WHAT?

Moving forward, my sister and I decided that we should meet annually. She still lived in Charlotte and I was in Omaha, so getting together had to be planned in advance! We decided that we should take a trip and have fun together.

Our trips together have become some of my favorite memories! We have spent time in other cities, or I have gone to Charlotte, as well as enjoying her visits to Omaha. I have cherished these visits as they are my opportunity to truly be with my sister and catch up and laugh.

Go Big Red!
2008.

Thanksgiving in Wahoo. 2014.

Brother/ Sister trip to Chicago. Billy Joel at Wrigley Field. 2017

In addition to having fun, we were productive. We started to ask each other deeper questions about what we remembered from the past. As we dug deeper and asked more questions, we decided to reach out to extended family members such as my dad, aunts, and my grandmother. We also reached out to my parents' friends who had babysat us when we were younger. We then asked members of Melyssa's family, the Brandts, about their experiences as she came into their lives as well.

During our conversations with friends and family, we asked them to share what they remembered about the period when our family was together. We also asked questions about anything they might have been involved with specifically. Through these conversations, the pieces of the puzzle started to come together. It was shocking to hear them explain what they had seen and heard. It also hurt to know that this information had been available all along, but we hadn't known enough to ask. We had also let the past stay in the past because hadn't expected to be reunited and have the chance to piece things together. As we took notes, we agreed that we should do something more than filling a notebook. The seeds of this book were sown, and that is how the writing process began.

At this stage, we would write about the research we conducted that ultimately led to the book in your hands. While some of the information may be interesting, my focus is on what this project has done for us. To be more specific, it has been cathartic to learn specifics about our past that we didn't know and then compile the information to create a book.

I'm not going to lie and say that it was easy. Far from it. In fact, forcing ourselves to go back and revisit memories has been very painful. There have been days when I didn't want to think about the past anymore. Even though portions of the research and writing journey were hard, it has also led to many good things as well. Personally, it allowed me to put certain things to rest. I mentioned that the priest I had spoken to had guided me to the prayers for the deceased. He showed me how I could continue to pray for my mother even if I hadn't come to a point where I felt peace. Well, he was right. Through those random prayers over the years and throughout the discussions with my sister, I came to a level of forgiveness that I hadn't allowed before.

I can't change what happened to our family. I can't bring back the twenty-four years of separation between my sister and me. There is no way that I will ever understand how both of my parents reached the conclusion that removing my sister from our life was going to help any of us. I have carried anger, shame, sadness, confusion, and guilt within me for so long. The weight of all those feelings and thoughts became too heavy for me to continue carrying. Instead, with my sister's help, I have been able to release that burden from my shoulders. I have forgiven my parents, but I will never forget.

At this point, my family deserves 100% of my time and energy. In the process of talking with my sister and hearing how she felt about what happened, I was shocked. I felt that she should have been even angrier than I was. I had assumed that she would continue to be bitter about what had happened to her. Instead, she was calm about the past and confident about where she was going. I couldn't believe it. She had every right to hold anger within her heart, but she had chosen not to do so.

Melyssa told me that if she'd had the opportunity to visit my mother, the only thing that she would have said was, "I want you to know that I made it. I am fine and doing quite well." That's it. Her attitude surprised me and then it began to inspire me. She helped me to release some of my anger. I started to realize that I had been angry, and on top of my own anger, I was feeling angry for Melyssa, too! She showed me that I could let go of the anger.

During this time of reflection my parenting duties never stopped, of course! I'm so thankful for that. All of this has allowed me to view parenting through a slightly different lens. Having a nineteen-year-old and seventeen-year-old has provided parenting challenges that are continually new! I am watching them turn into an amazingly talented young man and woman, respectively. Conversely, having two children in grade school has allowed me to go back and approach things slightly differently. I can use experience as a guide now. Even with all of that, I still find myself wondering if I am making good decisions as a parent.

I also wonder what my parents would think of how I do things. It's easy to find motivational books, memes, or coffee mugs filled with positive affirmations. Many of them are messages about family, or more specifically, about a "found family" or "chosen family." You know, the ones like this: "Family isn't always blood, it's the people in your life who want you in theirs. The ones who accept you for who you are, the ones who would do anything to see you smile and love you no matter what."

Sometimes we take those sayings for granted. It is easy to read them, smile, and pass by quickly. The truth is that those sayings are valid. I don't need a sign on the wall stating it, though. I have lived it, and you may have done it, too.

We build our "families" in many ways. A perfect example of this is the Brandt family. During the years since Melyssa and I reconnected, many of Melyssa's visits back to Omaha were spent visiting me as well as spending time with the Brandts. As time went on, many of the visits were combined. Major holidays such as the Fourth of July or Thanksgiving have turned into great opportunities for my family to spend time with the Brandt family. Over the years as the family learned more about our story, we continued to build relationships.

To be honest, it was tough for me at first. When I heard Melyssa refer to Bob and Peg as "Dad" and "Mom," it was hard for me to accept. It may sound weird, but I was still carrying guilt, and seeing their close relationship was bittersweet. I was truly happy that things had worked out so well, but I also felt shame about what had happened. My parents had given up the roles of Dad and Mom for Melyssa. Over time, though, I realized that the Brandt family accepted me for who I was, too. They knew about the past, had taken Melyssa in, and had accepted our relationship.

One of the best ways to describe my relationship with the Brandts came from Tia, who is one of Bob and Peg's daughters. For a brief time, I cut her hair when I worked a few nights in a local salon. After one visit she was paying at the front counter when the receptionist asked her, "Are you related to Patrick?" Tia responded by saying, "Well, he is my sister's brother." The receptionist may not have understood, but it makes perfect sense to us!

The Brandt family has accepted me, as well as my family, and have continued to show us love. They have been a model of grace and love, and they have had an incredible impact on my sister's life. I am grateful for the role they have played in her life and how they continue to care for all of us.

The Brandt family, 2021

People have always seemed to step into our lives at just the right time. They have helped to patch cracks in our "cup" so that it can be filled time and again. They have helped us to become whole again. My sister is back. My friends are still there. My children and wife are by my side. The "in between" happened, but we are now whole again.

MELYSSA'S CLOSING

It wasn't easy writing this book. It was actually hard at first. I have never written anything like this before. Nothing since school at least.

It was a start and stop process. I would send portions to Patrick and then we would work together to get things to flow. I had to take many breaks along the way.

It was hard to write certain portions. Revisiting some of these moments in my life was painful. There were times when I didn't want to think about certain things that had taken place in my life. Some of the emotions that were attached to those memories are painful.

When I hit a wall, Patrick would find a way to encourage me. It kept me going, and we continued to find a rhythm to our writing style. To tell this story knowing that my children, family, and friends would finally know the truth scared me. Working together with my brother helped me to open up and feel safe when I shared these vulnerable thoughts. We were able to gain confidence and overcome fear in sharing our story.

It has meant so much for us to discover all the facts that we hadn't known as children and young adults. Patrick needed to know what I went through, and in turn I needed to know what he had gone through. Without knowing those things, it would have been easy to assume things were fine. I didn't know how much he struggled inside and how broken his family was. He needed closure to know what I lived through. This book has helped us both to achieve that.

As of this writing, Olivia has graduated from college and Albert is halfway to his degree as well. With them both out of the house, I have taken extra time to volunteer in a few ways. I spend time at a local soup kitchen, and I also support my family's foundation, The Brandt House, which serves families in need.

The Fleming family, 2021

People ask me why I like to volunteer so much. I think deep down it is my way of trying to help people to avoid having to wonder where they will live, or a way to help one person's life in some way. I faced some of those feelings while growing up, and I want to help someone else avoid that feeling.

The rest of my time is spent at the gym. I love the gym! Yes, there is a physical gain that I make by working out so much, but the gym has meant so much more. At my gym, you are accepted for who you are. I have formed strong friendships that began at the gym, and I cherish them.

I am so thankful that Patrick and I were able to tell our story. It is very hard when someone asks me a question about my past. One of the main reasons is that there is so much involved in answering it! Which part do you want to know?

I feel closer to my brother than I ever have, and I feel like we have closed a circle that allows us to move forward with a sense of pride. Thank you for reading and learning about our past!

Stronger than ever. 2023

PATRICK'S CLOSING

I agree with what Melyssa said. It wasn't easy to write this. I didn't know what it would take to write a book. We were determined, though, and just the act of telling someone else that we were writing a book kept us motivated. The more people we told, the more motivated we became to prove that we were actually doing it!

Finding time to write was one of the biggest hurdles. Once we got going, though, we found that the process of writing would ebb and flow. When we finally felt like we had it all down, the next step was editing what we had written. Writing isn't hard, but editing is!

I must tell you that this book is a true labor of love. It means everything to me. To be able to find out details that we didn't know and in the process to learn so much about each other has meant everything to me.

To have my sister in my life and to know that she will always be there is the best feeling in the world! I look up to her so much! She has inspired me and helped me to deal with how I have felt about my family. Her success and outlook on life has helped me strive to rise to that same level.

My time now is filled with my children. As of this writing, my son Sam is in his sophomore year of college, and Lily is close to graduating high school. Meanwhile, Vada and Charlotte are living their best lives in grade school. It is nothing short of inspiring to watch them grow into the amazing individuals they are. I beam with pride over them!

My wife is my anchor through all of this. I travel to teach and motivate people, while she gives me support from home. I couldn't do what I do without her help. Jenny has also been a huge support in the writing process! I am grateful to her for standing by me and lifting me when I needed it.

The Butler family, 2020

Finally, thank you for reading this book! Everyone faces challenges in their lives. Writing a book about them takes tremendous courage and confidence, and I appreciate you for taking the time to read what we have written.

"We are products of our past, but we don't have to be prisoners of our past."

ACKNOWLEDGMENTS

We are proud of what we have put together here. We are not professional writers, and it probably shows. We don't really care about that. We wrote this in our own words, and that was the most important thing to us.

We didn't set out to write a bestseller. We wrote this book for ourselves and for our families and friends. It took a lot of time to put it together, and we both agree that we are thankful that we did it! At times it was cathartic, and at some points painful! Well worth it, though! We had great encouragement along the way from so many family members and friends. Thank you all for motivating us!

𝒫

Lisa Pelto and the Concierge Marketing team - Our fearless publishing leader! We can't thank you enough for taking our vision and making it come to life! Your experience and guidance have been invaluable. We are grateful for all that you have done!

Janet Tilden - Our Editor. Your experience has shown through time and again. Thank you for allowing our writing voice to remain true while you gently nudged us in the right direction. I am in awe of your skill!

Melyssa - My sister forever. You have given me so much when I needed it the most. Your tireless energy and enthusiasm for life inspire me and countless others around you. Thank you for pushing to make this book a reality. Thank you for sharing and being vulnerable so that others can learn how fantastic you are. You are simply amazing, and I hope that when I grow up, I can be like you! I am eternally grateful for you. I love you.

Jenny - My amazing wife and partner on this journey. Thank you for being such a positive force in my life. I am so thankful that you walk next to me every step of the way. Your smile never fails to melt me! Thank you for taking my heart and never giving it back. Thank you for putting up with me and loving me for who I am. I will never shine as brightly as you do, but boy, do I wish I could! Thank you for being such an amazing mother to our daughters. They have a beautiful role model, and I am grateful for you. I love you.

Kim - Thank you for being the fantastic role model and mother to our children that you are. Kim, you are amazing! You have been nothing short of an all-star mother and example for Sam, Lily, and me. You and your extended family are truly inspiring, and I am grateful for all of you. Thank you for being such a fantastic partner to me. Our kids scored when they landed you.

Sam, Lily, Vada, Charlotte - My children. You are the greatest treasure in my life! You are my reason for being. Sam, my son, I love and respect the young man that you have become. I am so proud of you! Keep pushing for all that you want! You have continued to impress us with all that you do! You will make good things happen, son! Lily, ahhhh my Belle! I burst with pride as I watch you continue to shine! My golden girl can do it all! You inspire me daily! There are no limits for you! Go after it all! Don't stop pushing. I want everyone to see how amazing you are! I love you so much, Lily! Vada, my sweet girl. Your heart is so pure. You are so smart and thoughtful, and I am so proud of all that you do! You are so much like your mother, and it is beautiful to see! Keep pushing, sweet girl, you are going to do so much! Charlotte, my little one! Well, not so little now, but you will always be my baby. You have grown into the funniest and most caring girl. Remember what I said: "You are always in my heart, and I am always in yours!" I love you, sweet girl!

W.C. - My brother in life. The godfather to my sweet Lily. You have always been there for me, and I am truly a better person for having you by my side. You have shown up time and again, selflessly giving anything that you can. There is only one "W.C.," and I am so lucky that we have shared our lives

ACKNOWLEDGMENTS   353

together in one of my longest and strongest friendships. You are the brother that I always wanted. We are together forever. I love you, man.

Gerilyn - My sister in life. Oh, where to begin. Again, one of my longest-standing friendships in life. Gerilyn, I am so thankful for you. My God, the laughs we have had together! Good music and dancing? Count her in! You have been a role model to me since we were in high school. You continue to be one to this day. You provide such an outstanding example to everyone around you. An amazing mother, wife, sister, daughter, educator, friend. You handle everything that you do with such grace and a grounded sense of humor. Thank you for walking with me on my journey. Love you for that! I am forever grateful!

Lee and Mark Huebner - My in-laws. Thank you for showing me love and acceptance when I joined your family. Lee, you are truly the model of unconditional love. Our girls love you and for good reason! You are an amazing grandmother, mother, and friend. I am so thankful for your presence in my life!

Greg - My first friend. Man, you were there when we were growing up, and even though we don't get to connect as often these days, I will always be thankful for you and your family. I love that we can pick up a conversation and let our sarcasm shine without fail. You were there from the get-go, and I will never forget it.

Tony - It just goes without saying…over thirty-three years and counting. The most authentic person anyone could ever find. Tony, you have been there for me, and we have seen some shit. The world only gets one Tony, and usually the world can't deal with that! Man, you have stood by me and never judged. You are family, and I thank you for making me part of yours. I will always stand loyally by your side, brother.

The Long family: Dan, Karen, Kelsi, Kirbi, and Kaitlin - The family who took me in. I have had the honor of handling the hair upkeep for your family for thirty years! More than that, though, I have been blessed to call you my good friends. Each month I walk into your home, and I feel like I am walking into my own home thanks to you. We have attended weddings, graduations, and rejoiced in the birth of babies in our families. You have treated me like a son in your family, and I am so grateful. You are the picture of a loving family, and I thank you for making me part of yours.

Colleen Quinn - The mother we all wished that we had. Thank you for giving a skinny guy a chance to be a doorman! It allowed me to see a world that I am so grateful for. Colleen, you are simply the best. There is always a smile to be had when you enter the room, and we all feel it. You continue to lift me up every time I see you. It always fills my cup, and I am a better man (with a better sense of humor!) for having your influence in my life. Thank you, my friend. I am so grateful for you!

Jesse - My brother in life. Thanks for always being there, man. Through many moves and countless ups and downs in our lives, you have been there. I can't thank you enough for your continued friendship. So many endless conversations about football, music, and life. I couldn't have those with anyone else. Find the River.

More of my circle - Your "chosen family" plays such a vital role in your life. My circle of friends has lifted me up so many times. I am grateful for all of you. Marta, work brought us together and friendship, weddings, children, and many laughs followed. I continue to look up to you! Megan, isn't it funny how work brings people together? So many talks about work, family, and parenting. You are an inspiration to me! Dina, our high school friendship has stood up over time. Thank you for your friendship as well as for the outstanding photos. Your talent shines just like you do! Justin, man, you have pursued your passion and shown us how it is done. I continue to be envious of your talent. I need to return to MKE!

Ryan Wilkins - Thank you for your continued encouragement during the writing process! Also, big thanks for "proofing" and giving suggestions. Your boundless enthusiasm and support have meant so much!

Stephanie Kocielski - You gave me the kick in the pants that I needed! The manuscript may not have been finished by November 13th, but it got done in the end! Stephanie, you helped me to get centered and to put myself first. Our talks are gold! You helped me to "save the space." You are one of the most authentic people I know. Thanks for keeping me focused. You are a gem, my dear.

Mary Moeschler - Thank you for proofreading and supplying your edits! They were pure gold and a tremendous help! I feel our relationship came "full circle" when you walked through the door at Peg and Bob's! It was a blessing to have your expertise and talent on our side. A sincere thank you!

Bands - The soundtrack to my life story. I could fill this book with music thanks to you. Instead, I will quickly thank The National, R.E.M., Van Halen, The Stones, Pixies, The Lone Bellow, Madonna, The Replacements, The Beastie Boys, and thousands of other bands for literally being my constant salvation.

M

Prudy - Where to start? Our relationship was like a roller-coaster that was filled with emotional ups and downs. I will never forget our first encounter when you held me in your arms and consoled me as I cried. Neither of us knew what was going to happen to me, but you were committed to helping me. After that, you definitely weren't the first person that I wanted to see coming through a door because it meant that I was going to be moving. Later, you disappeared for ten years, only to reappear when I was in one of the lowest places in my life. I found out that you weren't supposed to have contact with me, and then when I hit the bottom, you stepped back in at the right time. You were the only constant in my life through that entire stretch, and as I look back, I realize one thing: You always wanted the best for me. I wish that you were here to read this book. I can finally share the story where you played a major role! You were more than a caseworker; you became my friend. I'm so thankful that you agreed to walk me down the aisle so that you could "give me away" one final time. This time it was a happy occasion! I wouldn't have had it any other way. I wish that I could call and hear your voice one more time, or send you flowers like I used to. I love you, Prudy, and I miss you so much!

Mom and Dad - Wow, where to start…Dad, when you met me, I wouldn't look at you, let alone talk to you, yet you came back to the hospital and tried again. Your family life was chaotic at the time, but both of you decided to bring me into your house. I didn't make good choices with situations along the way, but you never abandoned me. You always showed me how to be a better person by working through things. I was different from the other kids because I was too old to adopt, but I knew in my heart that I wanted to be a Brandt. I was determined, and I will never forget the day when that finally happened. It was one of the best moments of my life. I finally had a family who was proud of me, and in turn, it made me proud to carry the Brandt name. You both have shown me love when I needed it the most, and you taught me how to love myself and how to love others. You also taught me so much about forgiveness. I still struggle with that, but I think I'm getting better! I'm so proud to call you Mom and Dad! Thank you for allowing me to be me, and for loving me unconditionally when so many others wouldn't.

My siblings - Tia, Tasha, Terra, Teresa, Tony, Cody, Brenda, Aaron, Alex, Nick, and Leigha. I am so lucky to have such amazing brothers and sisters! I will always be the oldest, and the last one, to become a Brandt. All of you have shown me what it means to be surrounded by love. Each of you has brought me such happiness in your own unique way! Thank you for giving me the "yes" vote to join the family! Each one of you has a special place in my heart!

Patrick - My amazing older brother who I look up to, seek advice from, and is always there when I need someone to just listen to me. I love your ambition to be the best you can be! It shows in your work and in your beautiful family. Thank you for pushing me to tell our story. There were times when it was very difficult, but you would tell me, "You got this!" and "Take as much time as you need." It always helped me to keep going. The night you picked up my phone call changed my life forever! I hate that we lost so much time, but I will cherish every minute that I have with you and look forward to many more amazing years of making memories! I love you so very much.

Big Al - I want to thank you for being the best dad to our two beautiful kids. They look up to you so much! You have stuck with me through everything and made me feel safe when I needed it. You continue to love me for who I am, and for that I am grateful. I know I don't tell you this enough, but I love you, and I'm so thankful for your love and support.

Olivia - You are beautiful, smart, and always impress me with how you keep going when things get hard. You are a survivor, and I love that about you. I am so proud of your accomplishments! You deserve so much happiness! I am proud to call you my daughter, and I love you to the moon and back!

Little Al - I love your drive for life! You are caring, funny, and always willing to help others. You are hardworking and it has shown with your amazing athletic skills! Underneath that, you are humble and kind and light up the room when you walk in. So many people look up to you and for good reason. I love you so much, and I'm proud to call you my son.

Berewick Beauties - You girls are the best! My time with you is always so great, and my face hurts from laughing and smiling every time I leave! You give me perspective on life, and we are always there for each other. I love all our deep conversations that cover anything we want! Thank you for allowing me into your beautiful neighborhood group. I love our diversity!

CrossFit Steele Creek - Lisa, I remember when I received an invite for a "meet-up dinner." After the dinner, I was floored when you invited me to join the group. You didn't even know me! That meant the world to me. This box has been one of the best things for me! I have met so many wonderful people. You created a space where people are kind and welcoming from the moment someone walks in the door. Our group doesn't care if the person is the most beautiful, most popular, or most fit. They are welcome because we care more about getting to know the person for who they are. That is a tribute to the great culture that has been created! The coaches are amazing, and 6:00 AM will forever be my happy place!

Cindy - My sweet friend. We had the best time together, and I will never forget how you supported me through the years. Those were wild and crazy times, and I will never forget you!

Kari - Thank you for taking me under your wing and helping to make my transition easier when I first moved to Wahoo. We had the best time together, and I will never forget how kind you were to me. You played a huge part in showing me what a real friendship can look like.

Kristy - To one of the best roommates ever! You were so fun and were there for me when I needed it the most! Thank you for always being a friend I could count on.

The Hinze family - You never forgot about me, and as you continued to look for me Facebook brought us back together. Even though I couldn't find you over the years, I never forgot about the impact you had on me. I am so thankful we reconnected. You helped me to put the pieces together about my story, and I will be forever grateful. I only wish that Jack and Jan could have seen that I found peace. I finally found a family that loved me just as much as they did. You will always have a special place in my heart.

Folly Girls - I can't imagine my world without you girls in it. You have shown me what true friendships are. I will never forget when y'all invited me to go with you on a "girls' weekend." You will never know how much that meant to me. I love you all so much and wouldn't change anything about our friendship for the world.

There are so many others who are also so important to me. I just want to thank you for making me a better person. Each one of you plays an important role in my life. I am so thankful, and I can't imagine my life without you.

PROMOTE AWARENESS
AROUND ADOPTION

Do you need a speaker for your next workshop, seminar, conference or retreat?

The authors are seasoned speakers and can customize and deliver compelling, thoughtful and motivating presentations for your group.

For more information,
visit www.MandPBondPublishing.com